AUDIO ACCESS INCLUDED

Classical Cello Duets

Arranged by Mr & Mrs Cello

Audio arrangements performed by
Massimiliano Martinelli and Fulvia Mancini (Mr.& Mrs. Cello)

Sound Engineering: Eustacc[illegible] [illegible]va, Matera

Photo by Ulrich Wydler

ISBN 978-1-70514-254-7

HAL•LEONARD®

Visit Hal Leonard Online at
www.halleonard.com

Contact us:
Hal Leonard
7777 West Bluemound Road
Milwaukee, WI 53213
Email: info@halleonard.com

In Europe, contact:
Hal Leonard Europe Limited
42 Wigmore Street
Marylebone, London, W1U 2RN
Email: info@halleonardeurope.com

In Australia, contact:
Hal Leonard Australia Pty. Ltd.
4 Lentara Court
Cheltenham, Victoria, 3192 Australia
Email: info@halleonard.com.au

Contents

Lullaby

By Bernhard Flies
Arranged by Massimiliano Martinelli and Fulvia Mancini

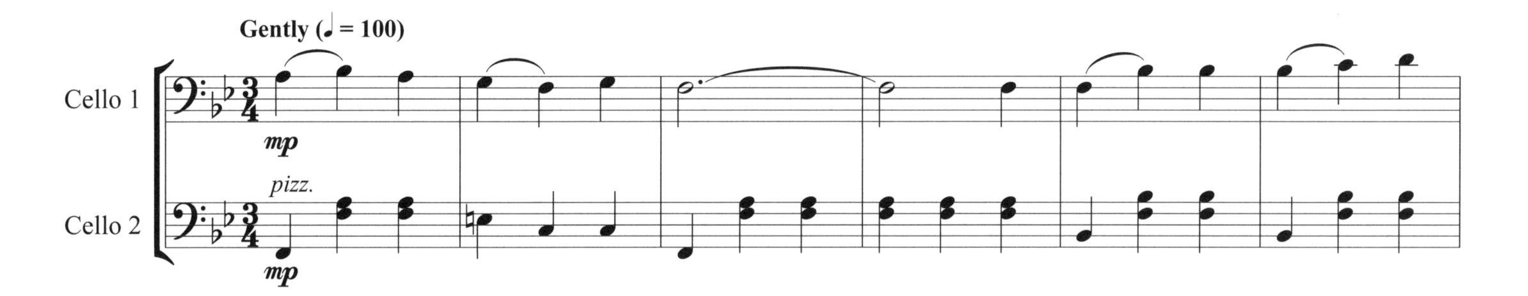

Lullaby

By Johannes Brahms
Arranged by Massimiliano Martinelli and Fulvia Mancini

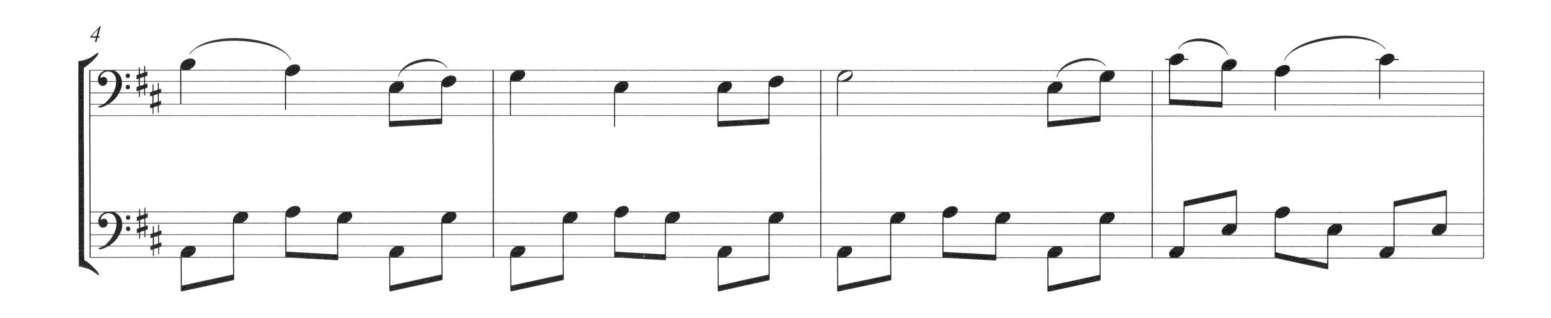

16
tr

20

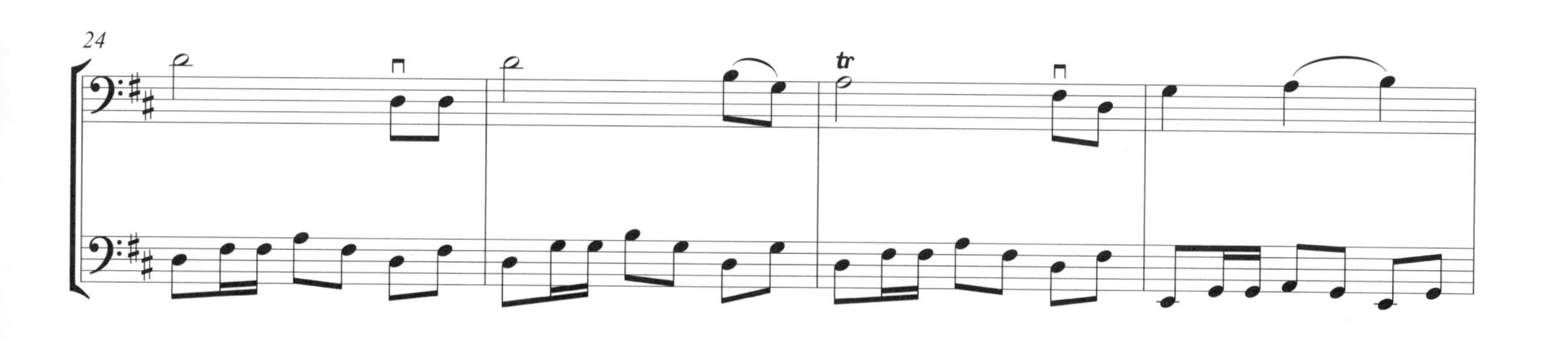
24
tr

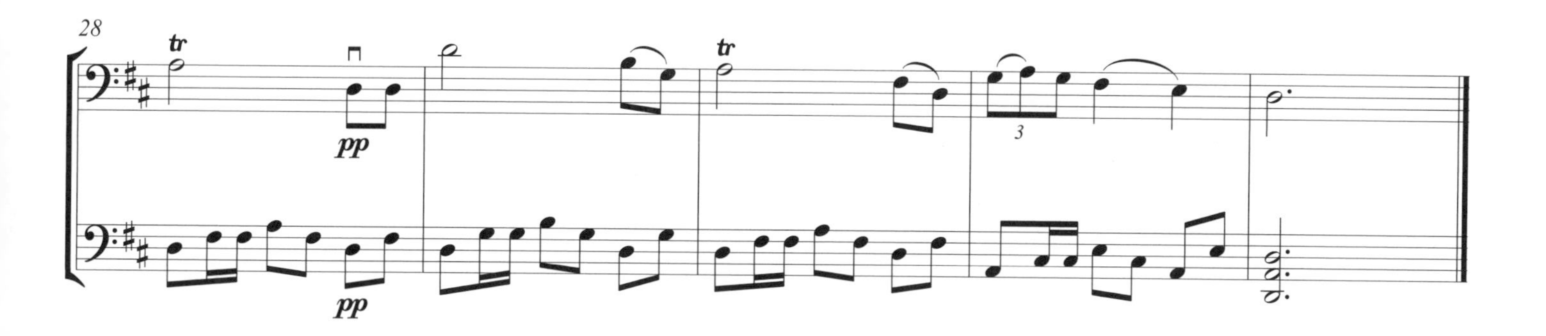
28
tr
pp
pp
3

Ode to Joy

By Ludwig van Beethoven
Arranged by Massimiliano Martinelli and Fulvia Mancini

Radetzky March

Op. 228
By Johann Strauss I
Arranged by Massimiliano Martinelli and Fulvia Mancini

21
mp

25

29

33
cresc.
dim.
cresc.

37
p
pizz.

41
f
arco
f

45

49
Fine

53

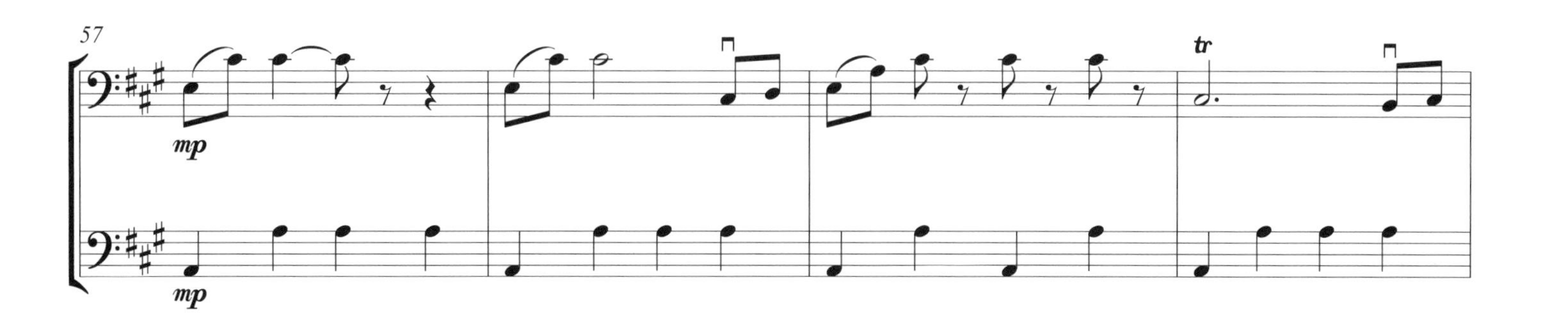
57
mp
tr
mp

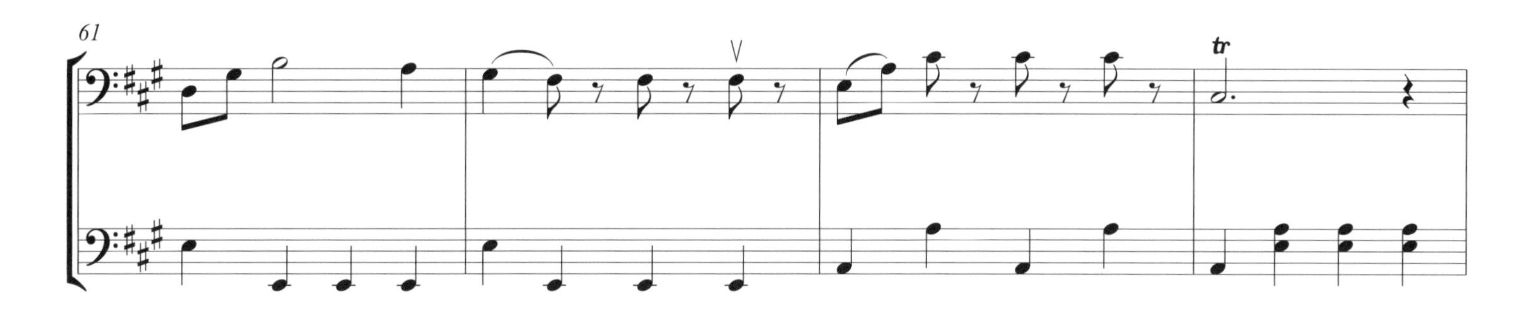
61
tr

65
tr

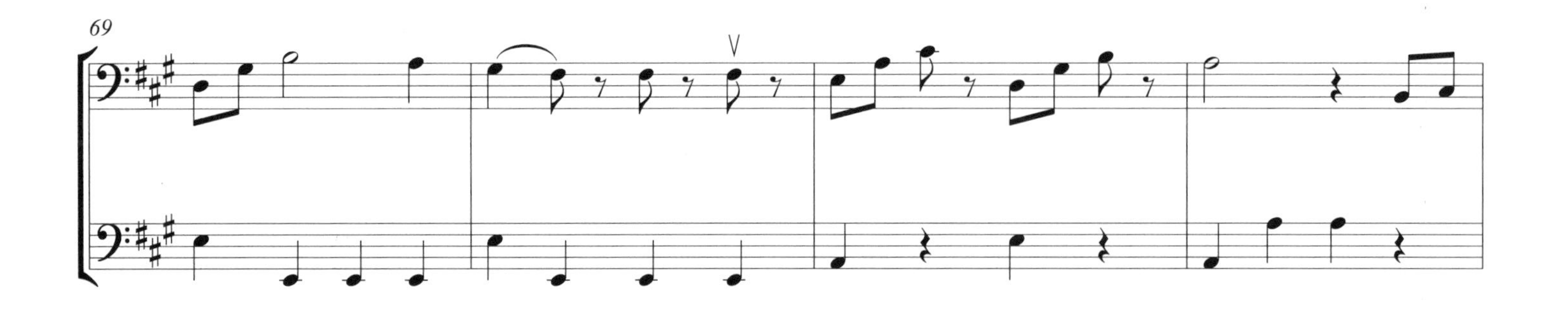
69

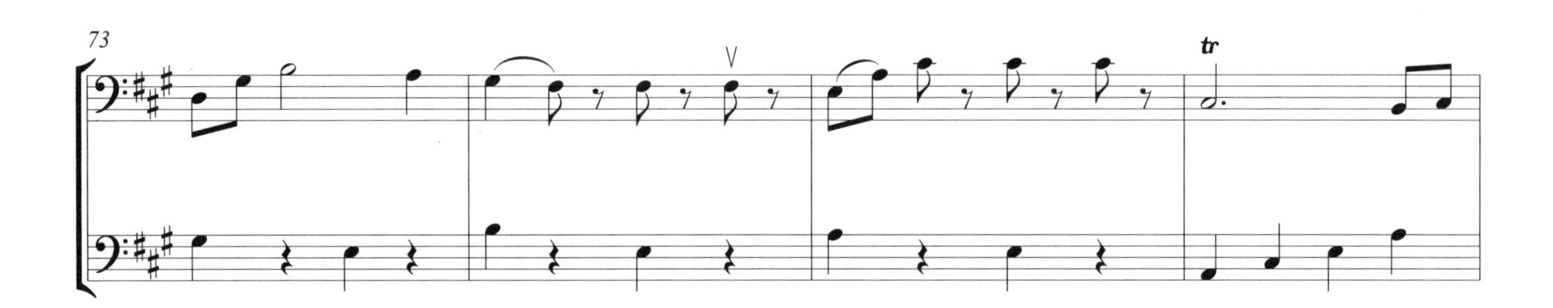
73
tr

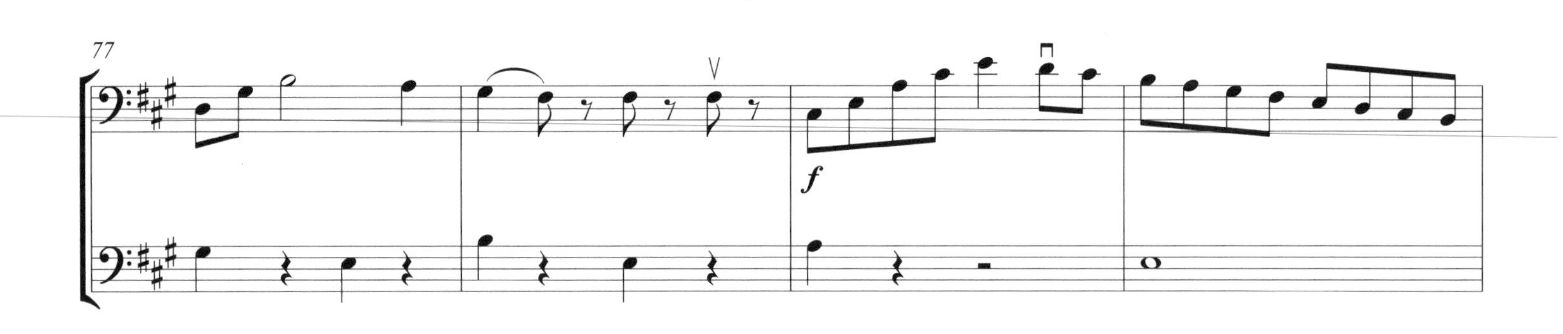
77
f

81
tr
pizz.

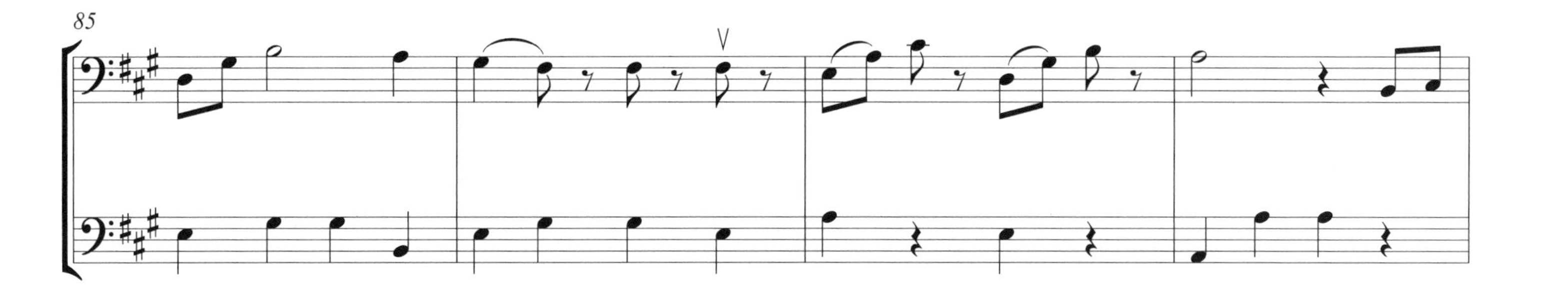
85

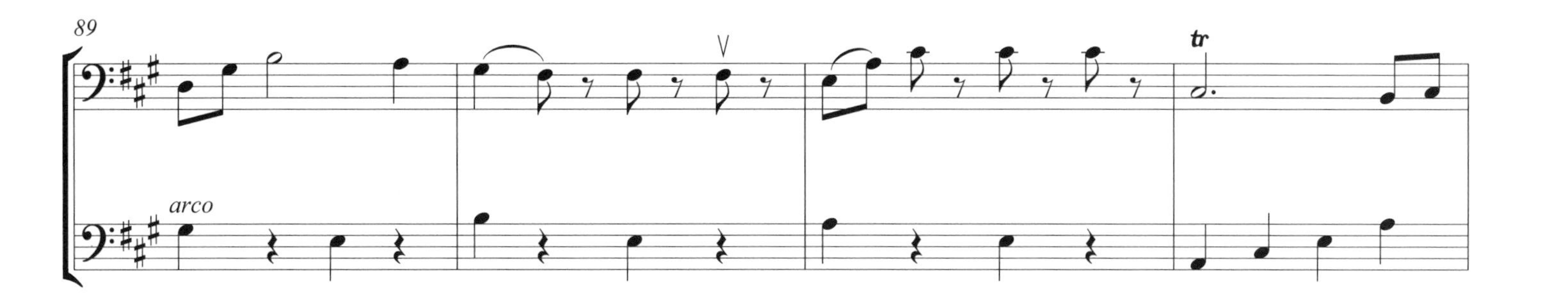
89
tr
arco

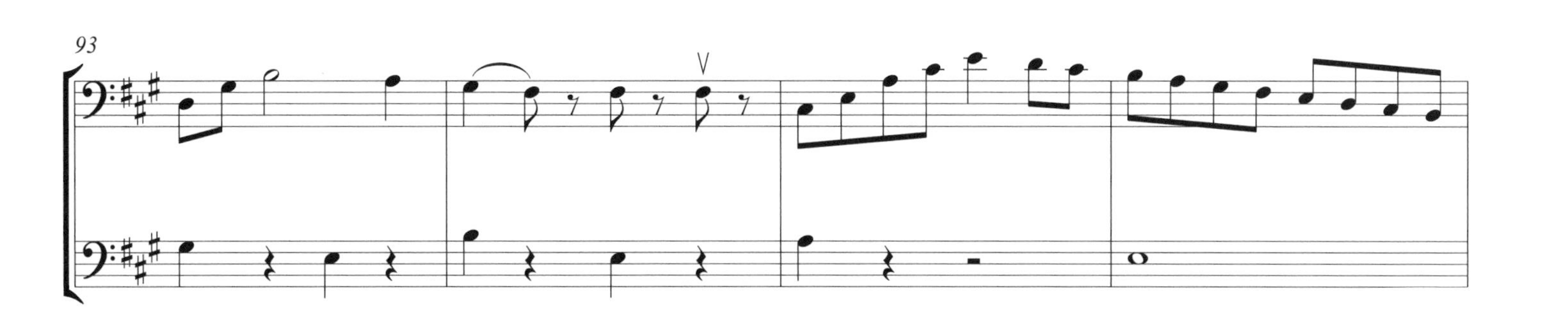
93

97
tr

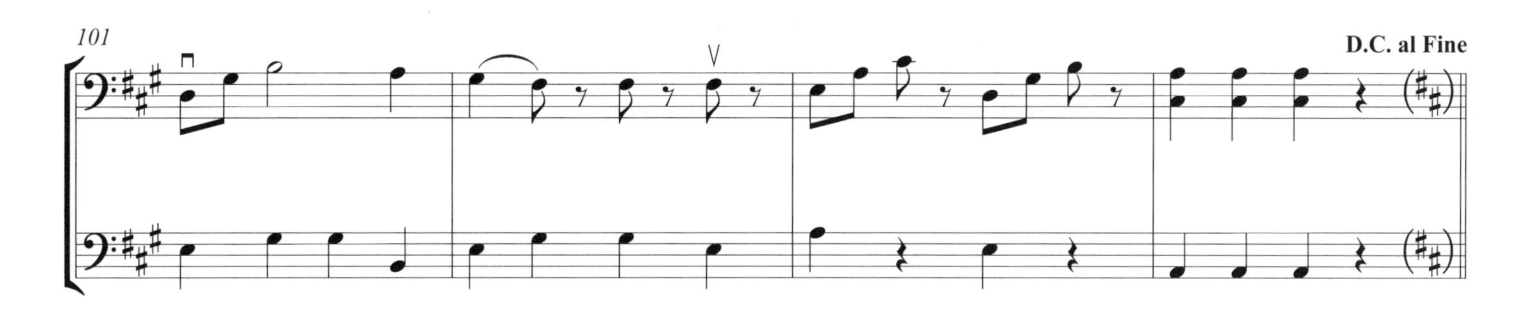
101
D.C. al Fine

Spring

from THE FOUR SEASONS
By Antonio Vivaldi
Arranged by Massimiliano Martinelli and Fulvia Mancini

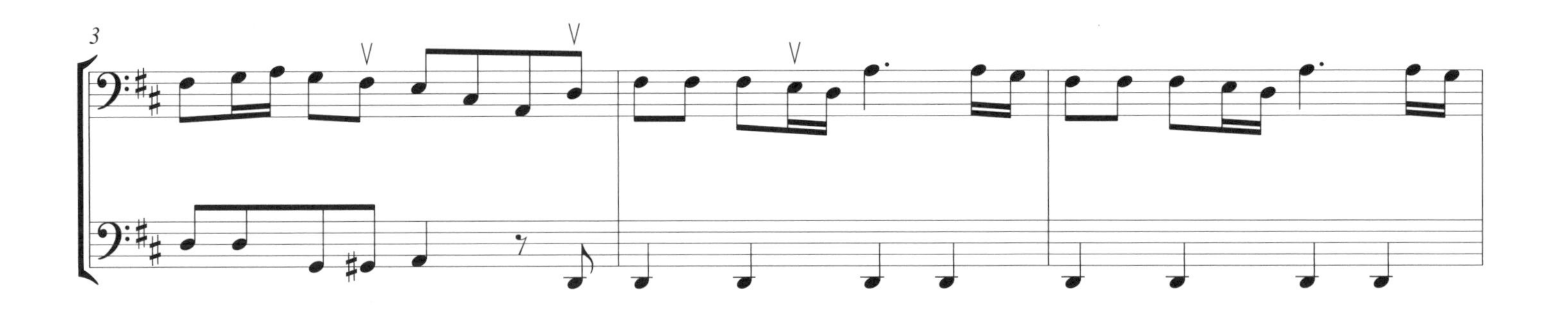

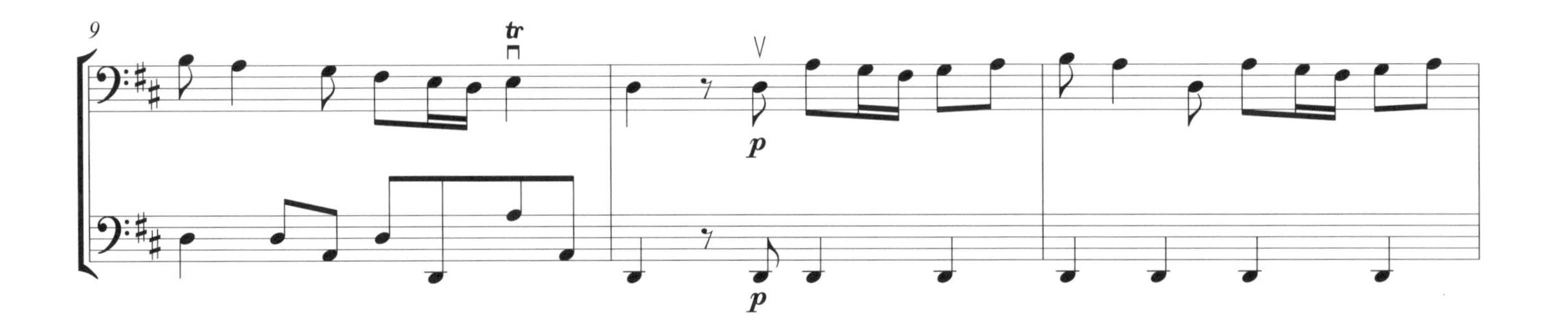

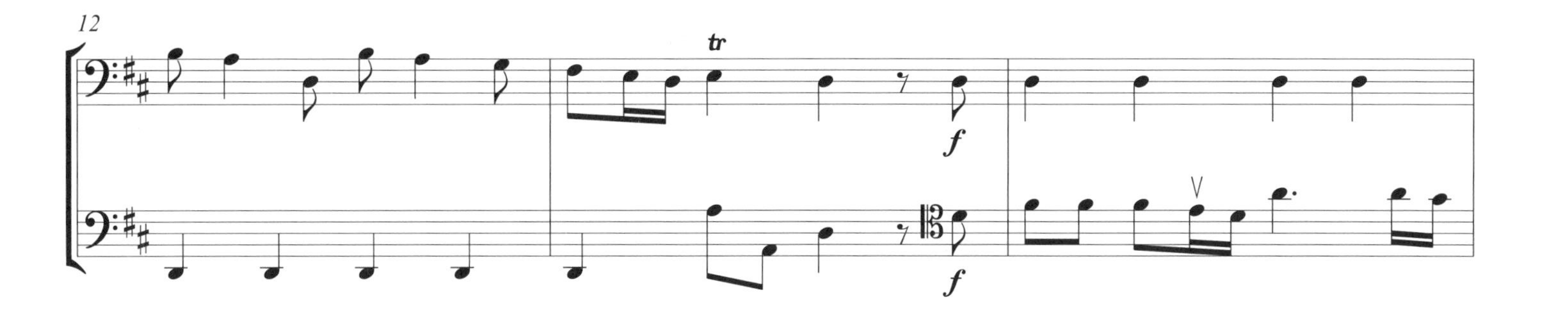
12
tr
f
f

15

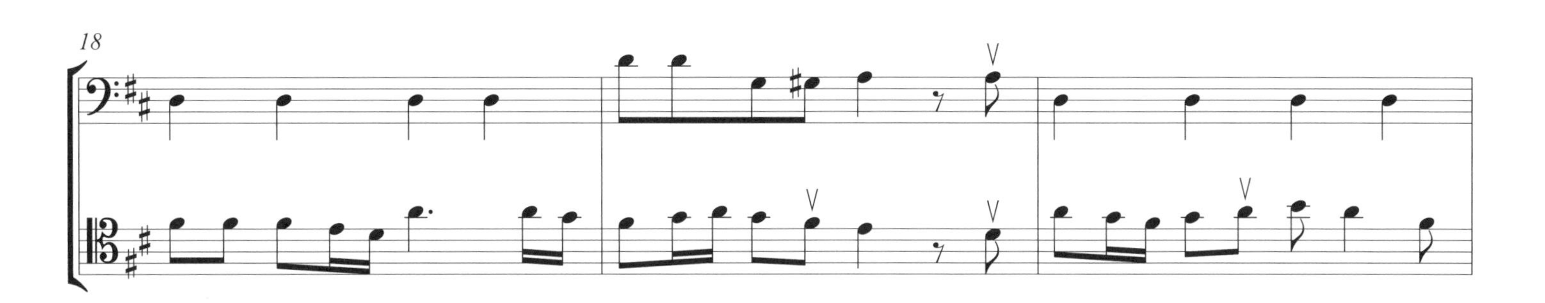
18

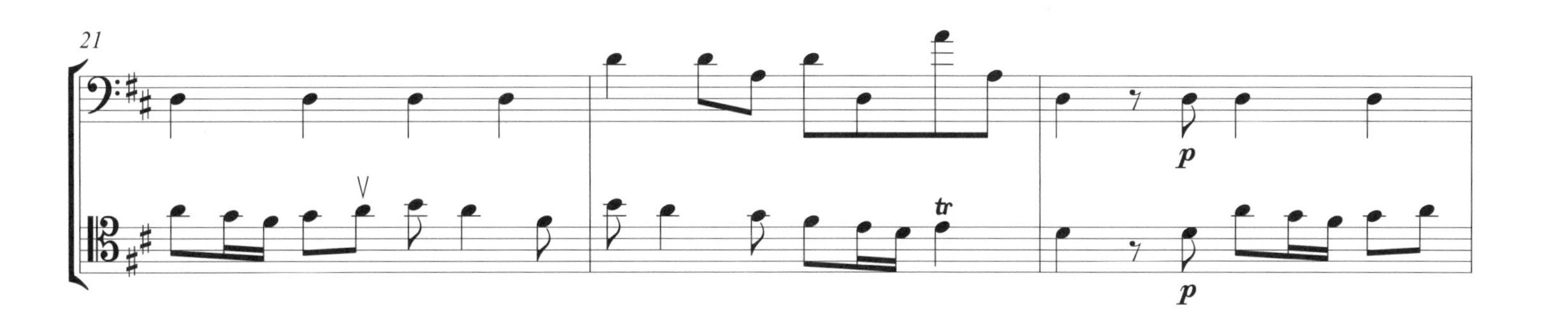
21
tr
p
p

24
tr

Waltz No. 2

from SUITE FOR JAZZ ORCHESTRA
By Dmitri Shostakovich
Arranged by Massimiliano Martinelli and Fulvia Mancini

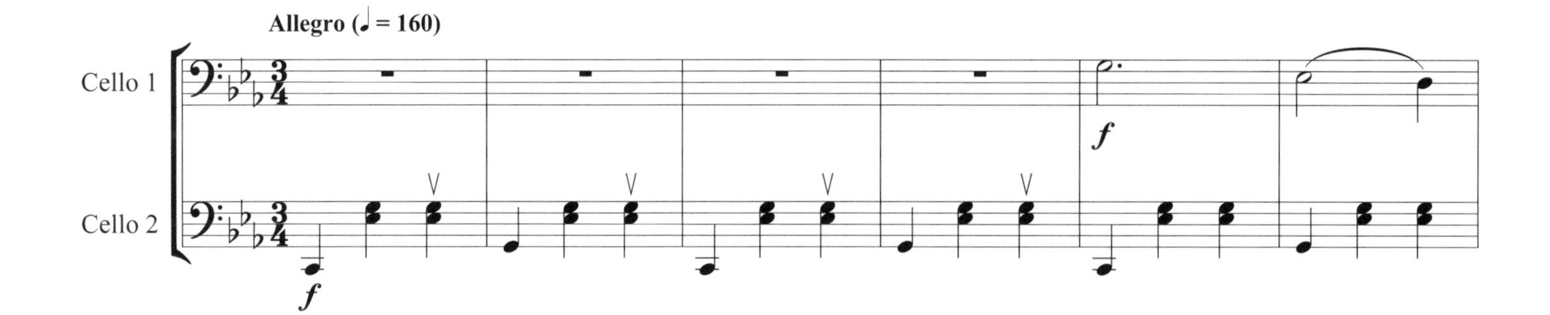

32

37

43
f
f

49
mf
mf

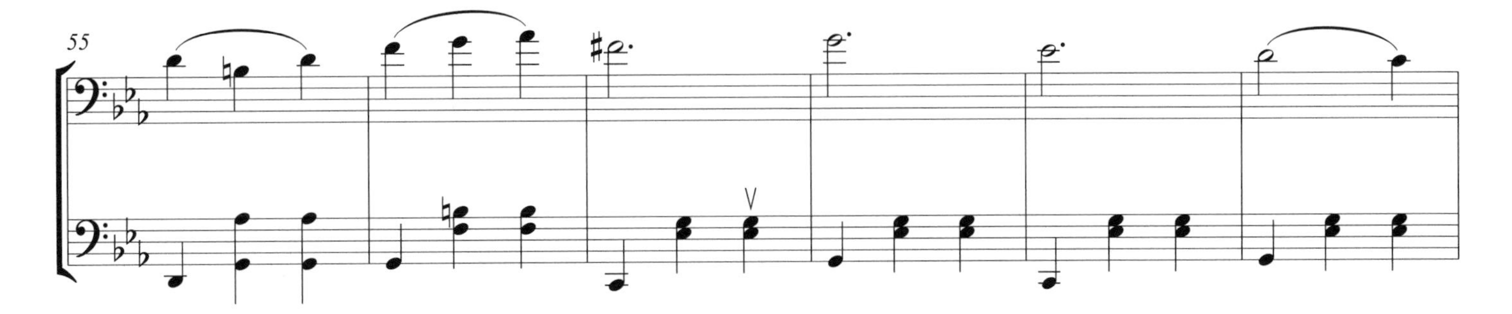
55

61
f

67
f

72

77
ff
ff

82

87

93

Lullaby

By Bernhard Flies
Arranged by Massimiliano Martinelli and Fulvia Mancini

Lullaby

By Johannes Brahms
Arranged by Massimiliano Martinelli and Fulvia Mancini

Ode to Joy

By Ludwig van Beethoven
Arranged by Massimiliano Martinelli and Fulvia Mancini

Cello 1

Radetzky March

Op. 228
By Johann Strauss I
Arranged by Massimiliano Martinelli and Fulvia Mancini

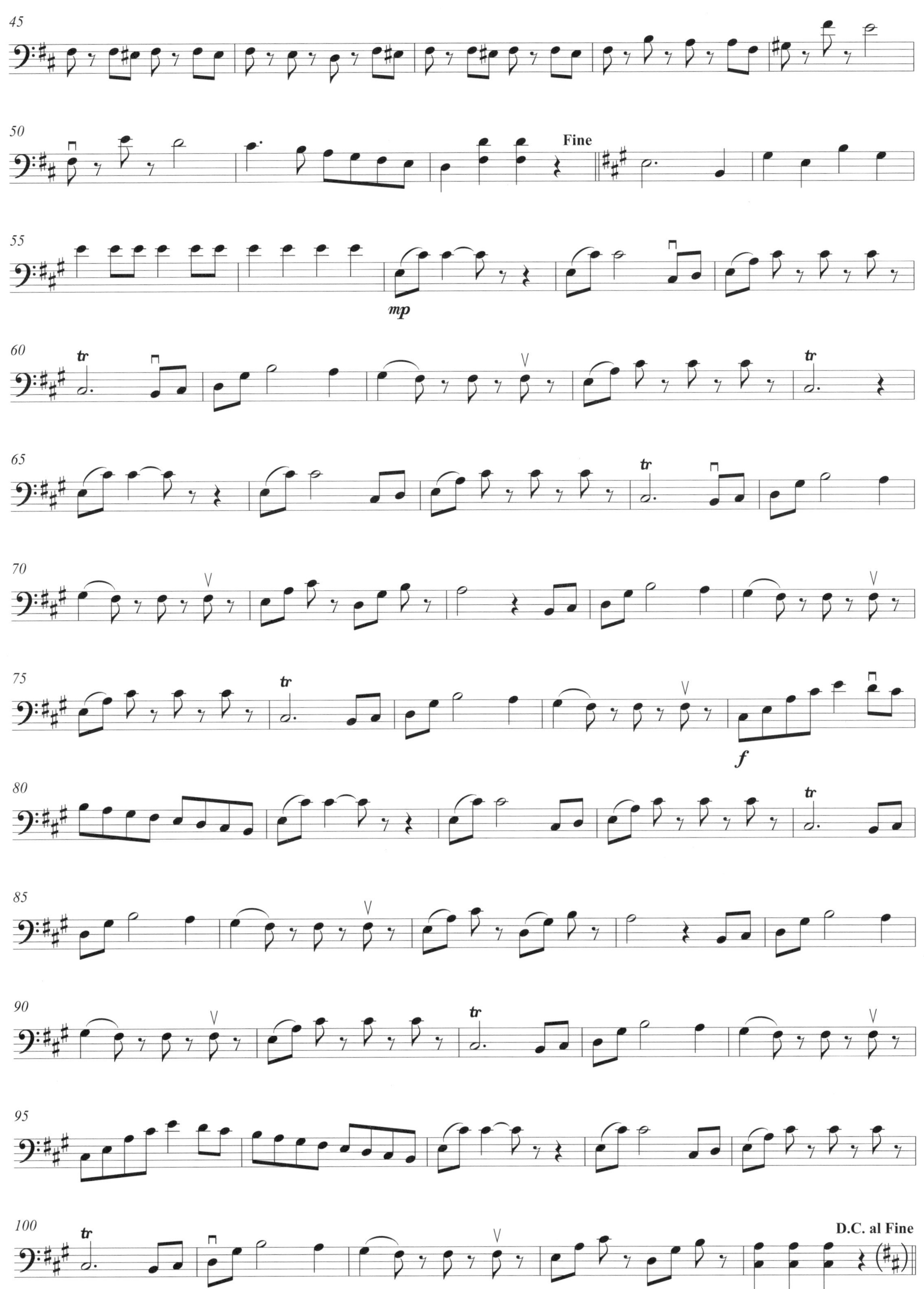
45
50
Fine
55
mp
60
tr
65
70
75
f
80
85
90
95
100
D.C. al Fine

The Swan

By Camille Saint-Saëns
Arranged by Massimiliano Martinelli and Fulvia Mancini

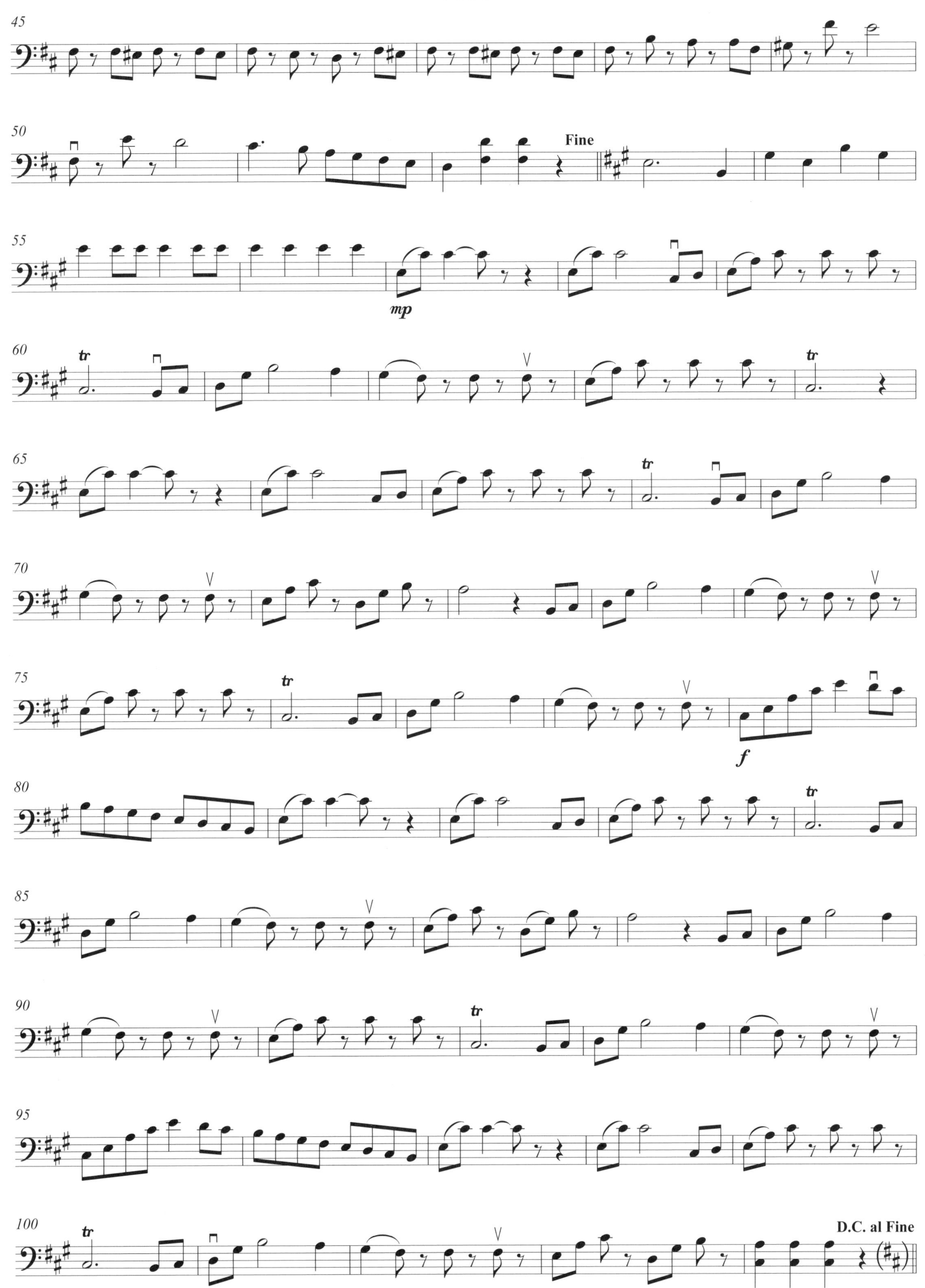

Fine
mp
tr
f
D.C. al Fine

The Swan

By Camille Saint-Saëns
Arranged by Massimiliano Martinelli and Fulvia Mancini

13
16
cresc.
19
21
(V)
cresc.
24
dim.

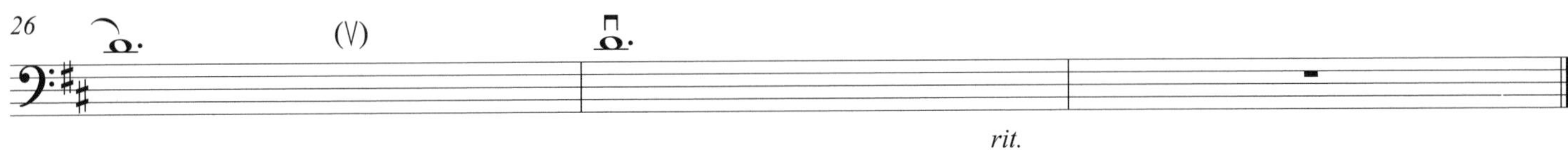
26
(V)
rit.

Va, Pensiero

from NABUCCO

By Giuseppe Verdi

Arranged by Massimiliano Martinelli and Fulvia Mancini

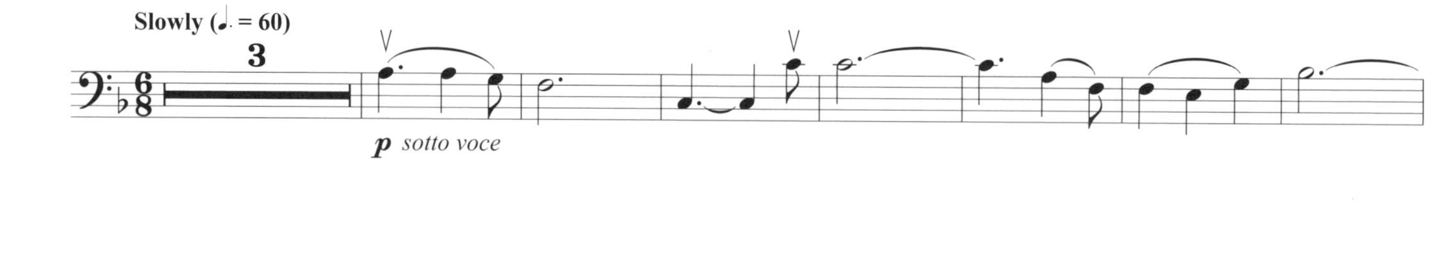

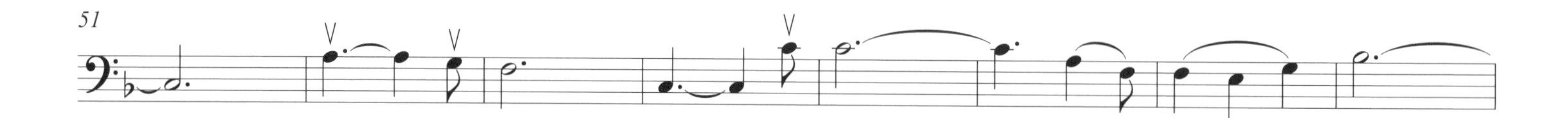

59
67
cresc.
f
75
dim.
mp
83
cresc.
f
91
mf
dim.
p
99
mf
107
mp
115
cresc.
f
dim.
pp

Cello 1

Waltz No. 2

from SUITE FOR JAZZ ORCHESTRA
By Dmitri Shostakovich
Arranged by Massimiliano Martinelli and Fulvia Mancini

78
ff

86

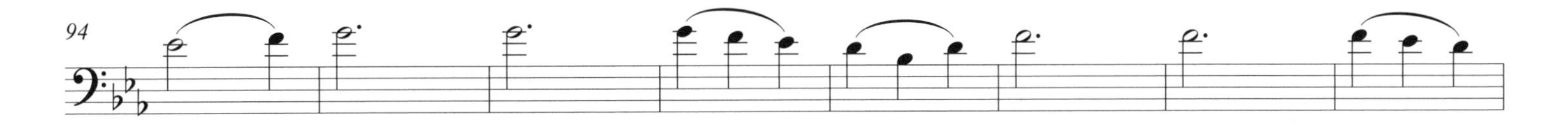
94

102
mf

110
f

118

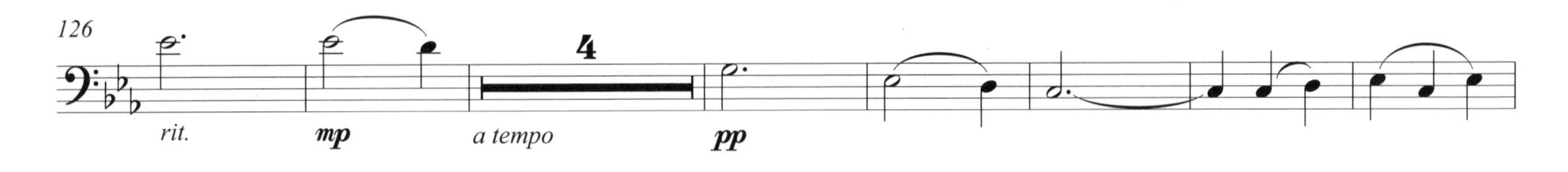
126
4
rit.
mp
a tempo
pp

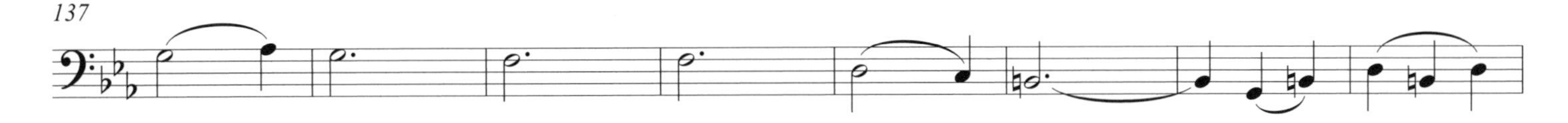
137

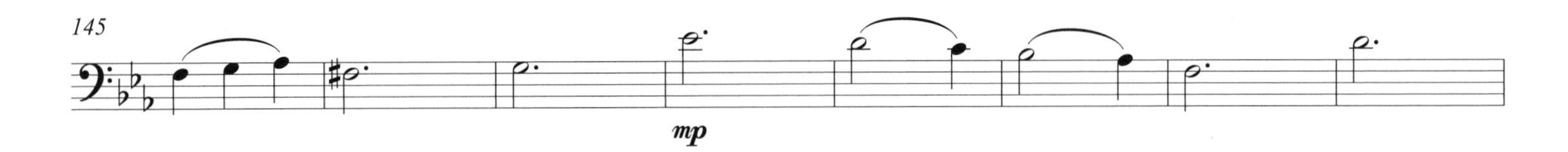
145
mp

153
p

161
mf
cresc.

Cello 1

Waltz of the Flowers

from THE NUTCRACKER
By Pyotr Il'yich Tchaikovsky
Arranged by Massimiliano Martinelli and Fulvia Mancini

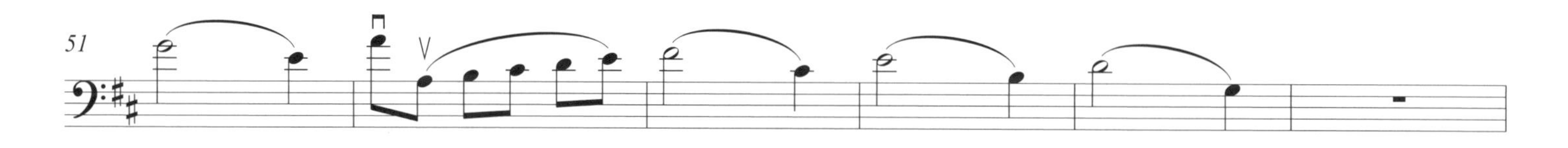

57
63
69
75
81
ff
87
93
99
105
111
2
p
118

William Tell Overture

By Gioachino Rossini
Arranged by Massimiliano Martinelli and Fulvia Mancini

37
42
47
52
57
63
68

73

Spring

from THE FOUR SEASONS
By Antonio Vivaldi
Arranged by Massimiliano Martinelli and Fulvia Mancini

Lullaby

By Bernhard Flies
Arranged by Massimiliano Martinelli and Fulvia Mancini

00369085

Lullaby

By Johannes Brahms
Arranged by Massimiliano Martinelli and Fulvia Mancini

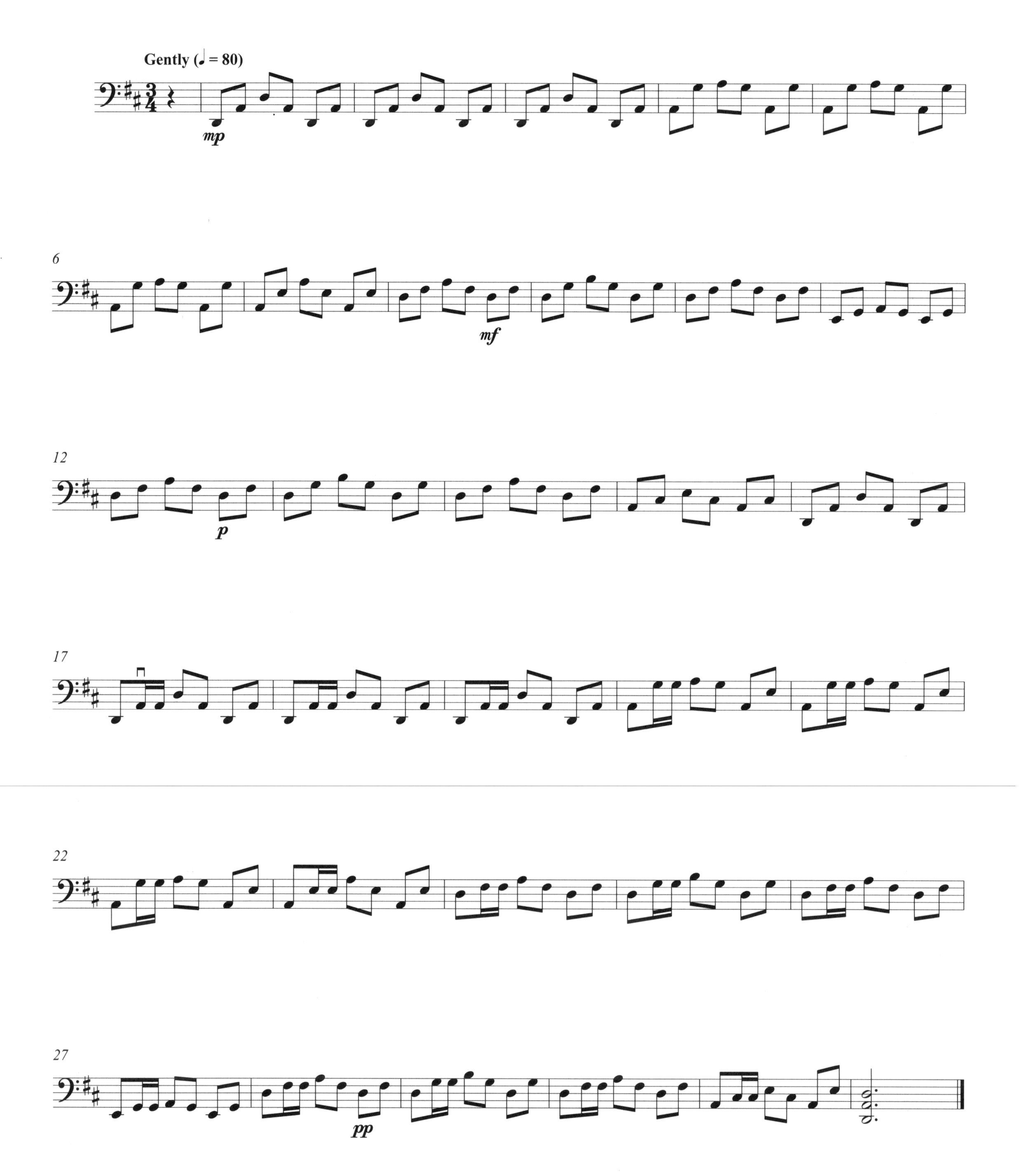

Cello 2

Lullaby

By Bernhard Flies
Arranged by Massimiliano Martinelli and Fulvia Mancini

Lullaby

By Johannes Brahms
Arranged by Massimiliano Martinelli and Fulvia Mancini

Ode to Joy

By Ludwig van Beethoven
Arranged by Massimiliano Martinelli and Fulvia Mancini

Radetzky March

Op. 228
By Johann Strauss I
Arranged by Massimiliano Martinelli and Fulvia Mancini

Ode to Joy

By Ludwig van Beethoven
Arranged by Massimiliano Martinelli and Fulvia Mancini

Radetzky March

Op. 228
By Johann Strauss I
Arranged by Massimiliano Martinelli and Fulvia Mancini

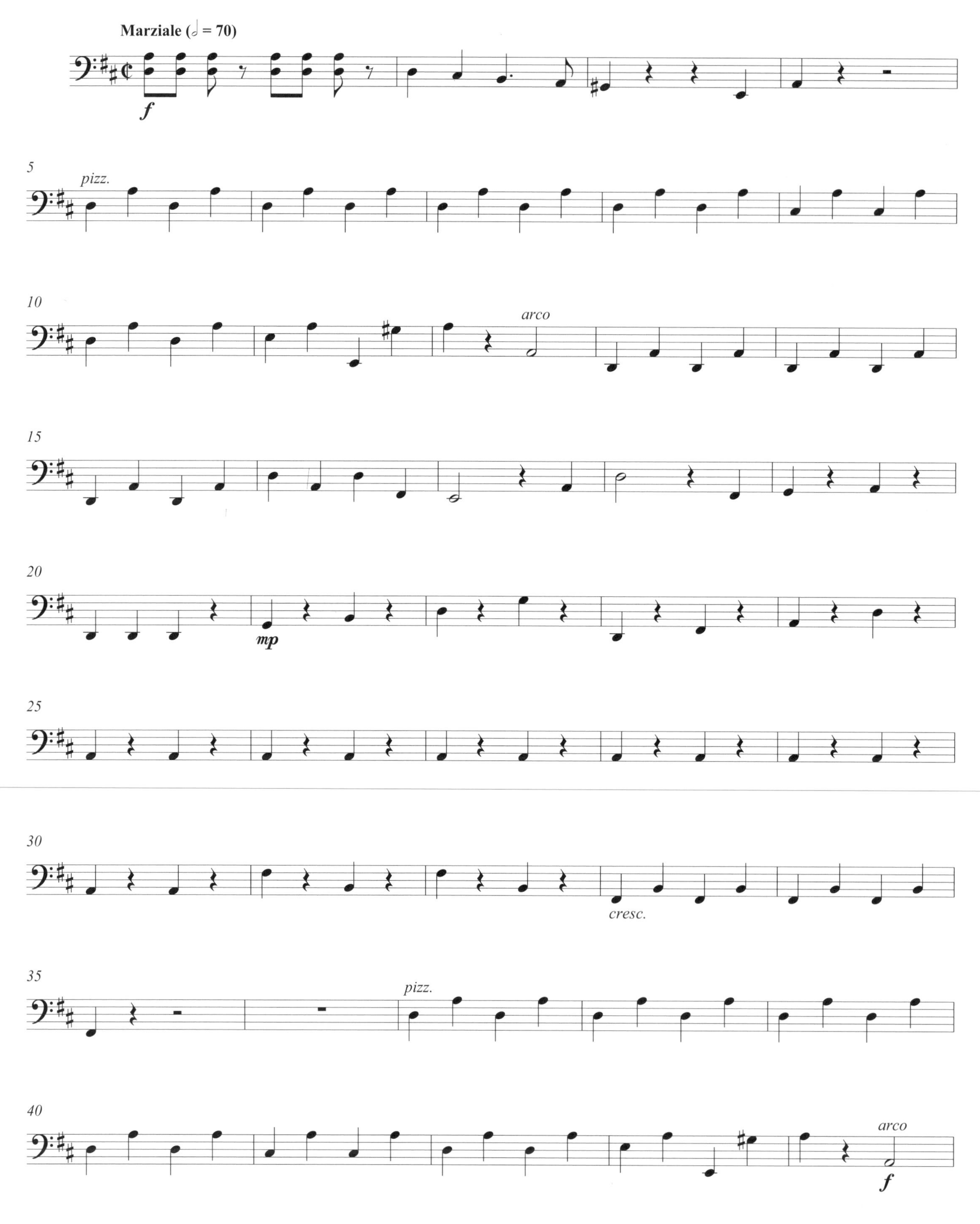

13

15

17
cresc.

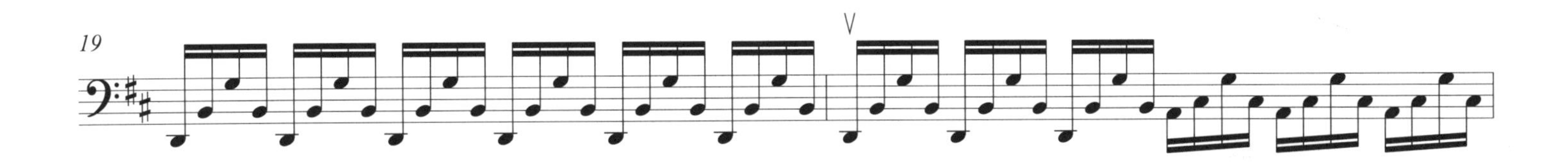
19

21
cresc.

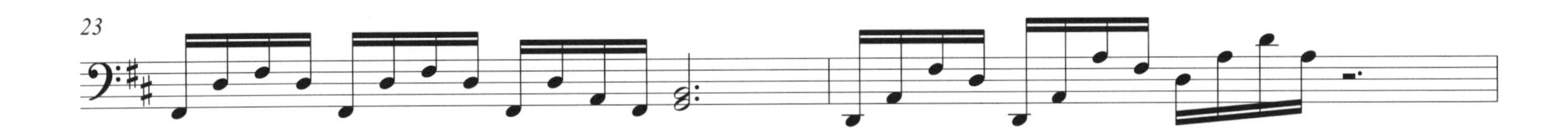
23

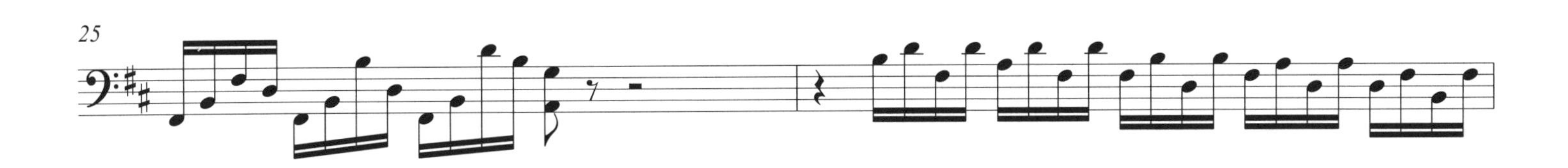
25

27
rit.

Cello 2

Va, Pensiero

from NABUCCO
By Giuseppe Verdi
Arranged by Massimiliano Martinelli and Fulvia Mancini

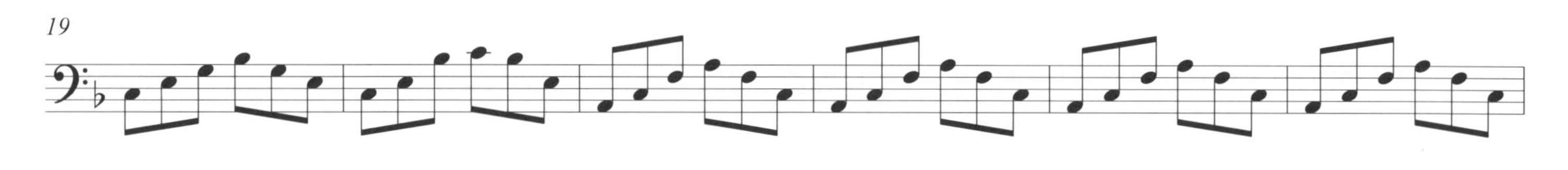

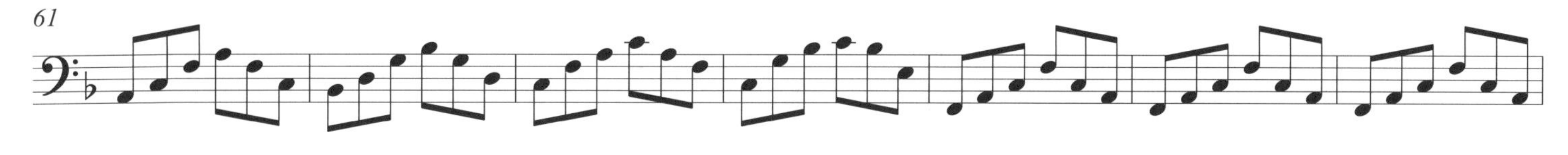
61

68
cresc.
f

74
dim.
mp

80
cresc.
f

86
mf

92
dim.
p

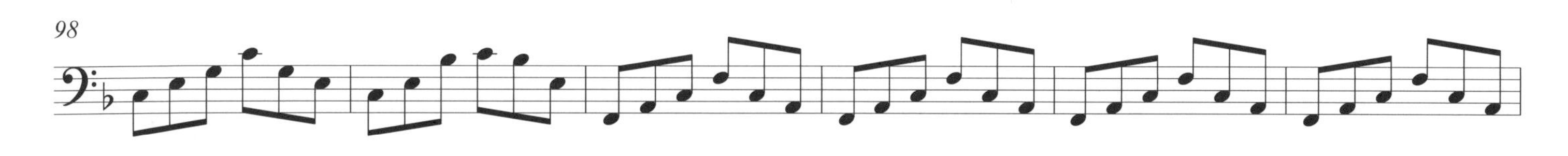
98

104

111
mp
cresc.

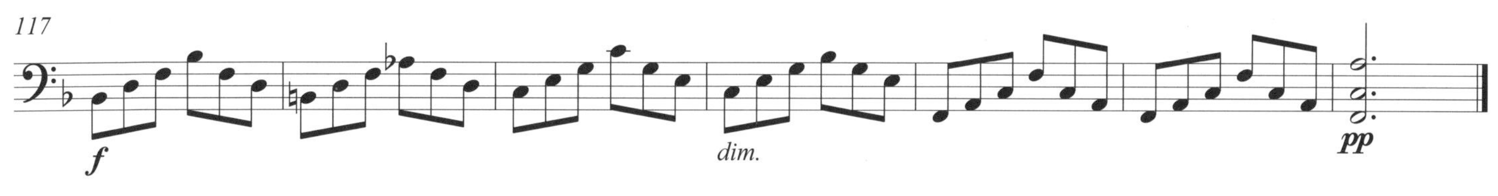
117
f
dim.
pp

Waltz No. 2

from SUITE FOR JAZZ ORCHESTRA
By Dmitri Shostakovich
Arranged by Massimiliano Martinelli and Fulvia Mancini

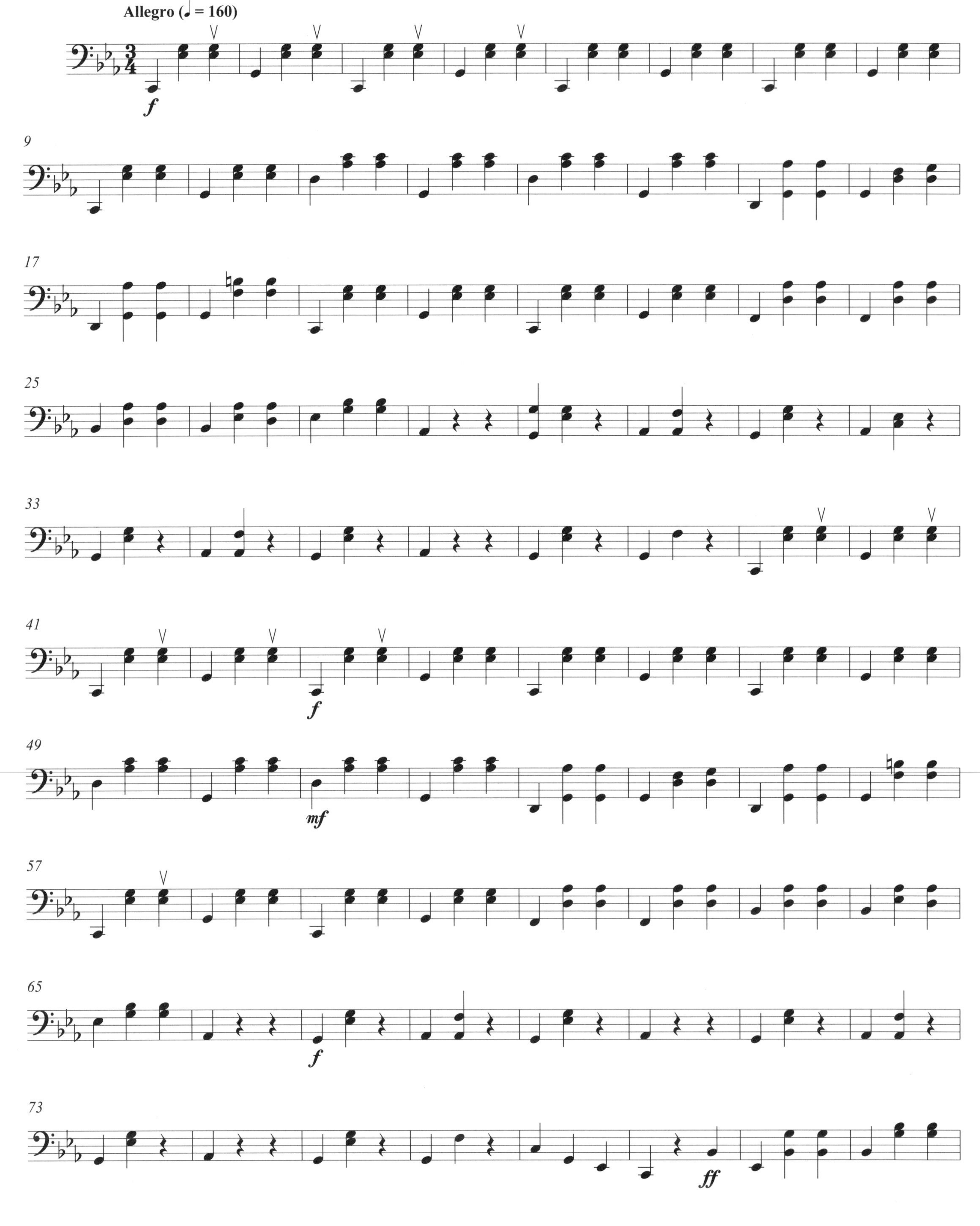

81
89
97
105
113
f
121
rit.
mp
f a tempo
129
dim.
pp
137
145
mp
153
p
161
mf
cresc.

Cello 2

Waltz of the Flowers

from THE NUTCRACKER
By Pyotr Il'yich Tchaikovsky
Arranged by Massimiliano Martinelli and Fulvia Mancini

55

61

67
dolce

73

80
f

86

92

98

105

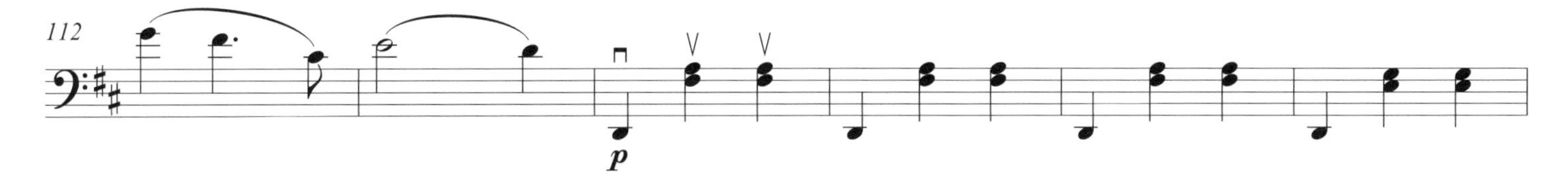
112
p

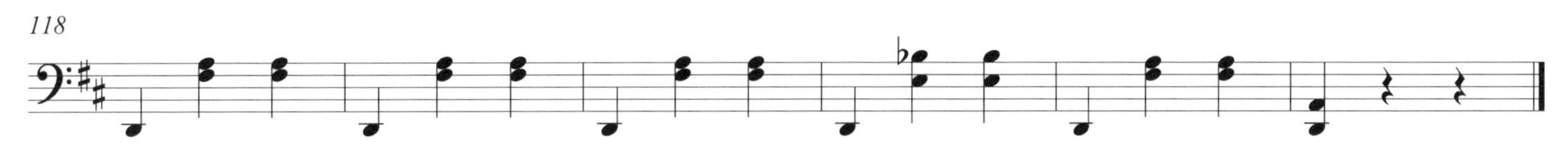
118

William Tell Overture

By Gioachino Rossini
Arranged by Massimiliano Martinelli and Fulvia Mancini

38
43

48

53

58

63

68

73

Spring

from THE FOUR SEASONS
By Antonio Vivaldi
Arranged by Massimiliano Martinelli and Fulvia Mancini

99
mf

105

111
f
f

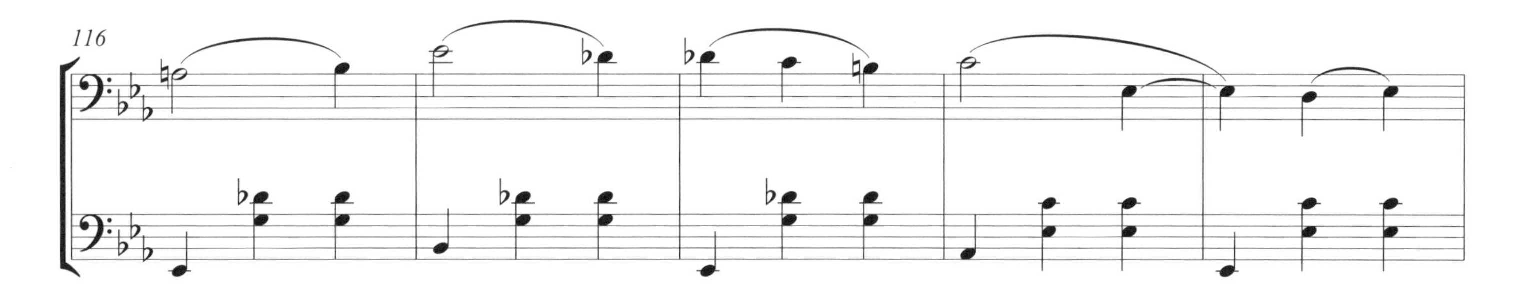
116

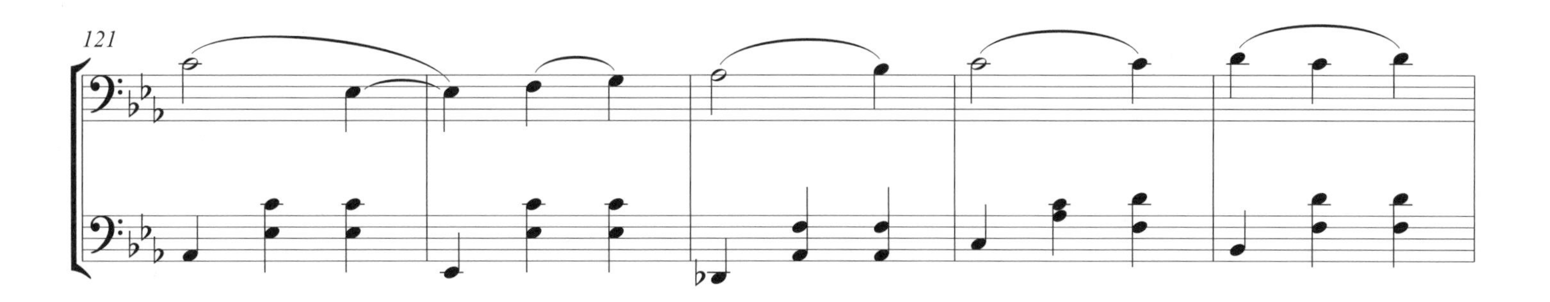
121

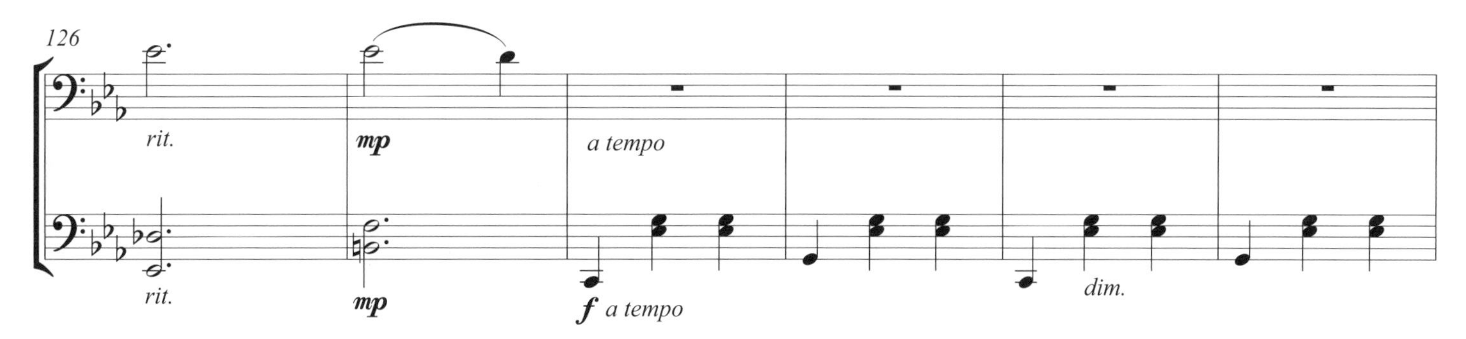
126
rit.
mp
a tempo
rit.
mp
f a tempo
dim.

132
pp
pp

138

144
mp
mp

150
p

156
p

162
mf
cresc.
mf
cresc.

The Swan

By Camille Saint-Saëns
Arranged by Massimiliano Martinelli and Fulvia Mancini

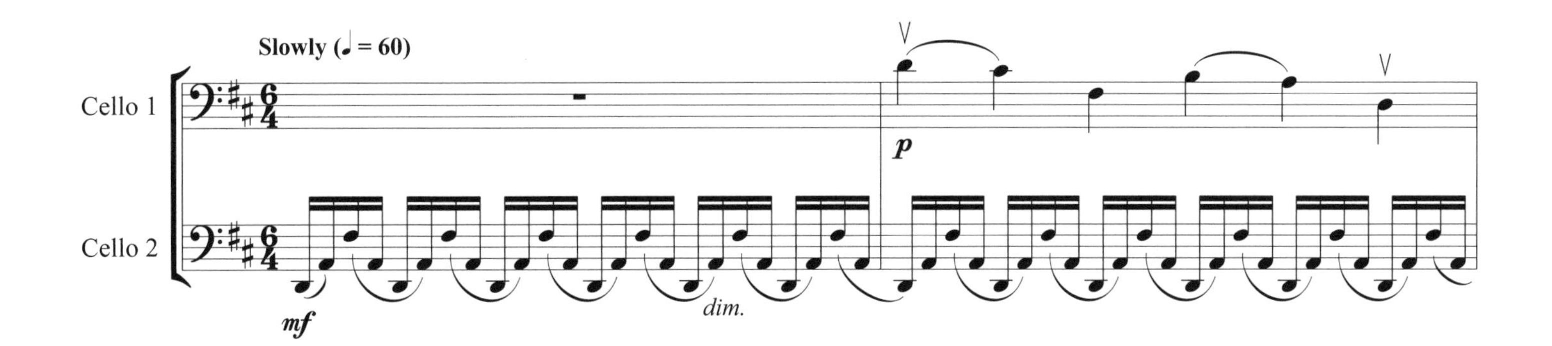

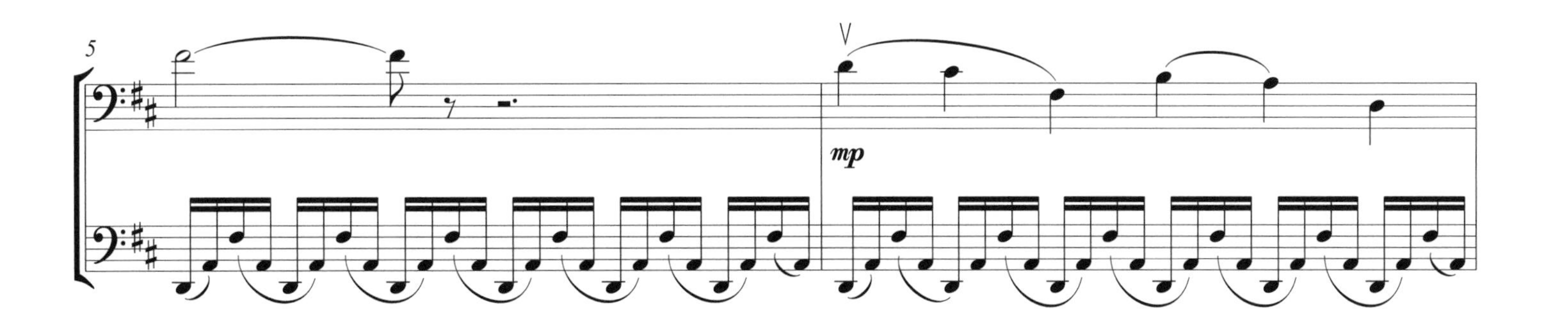

9
f
mf
f
mf

11
mp
mp

13

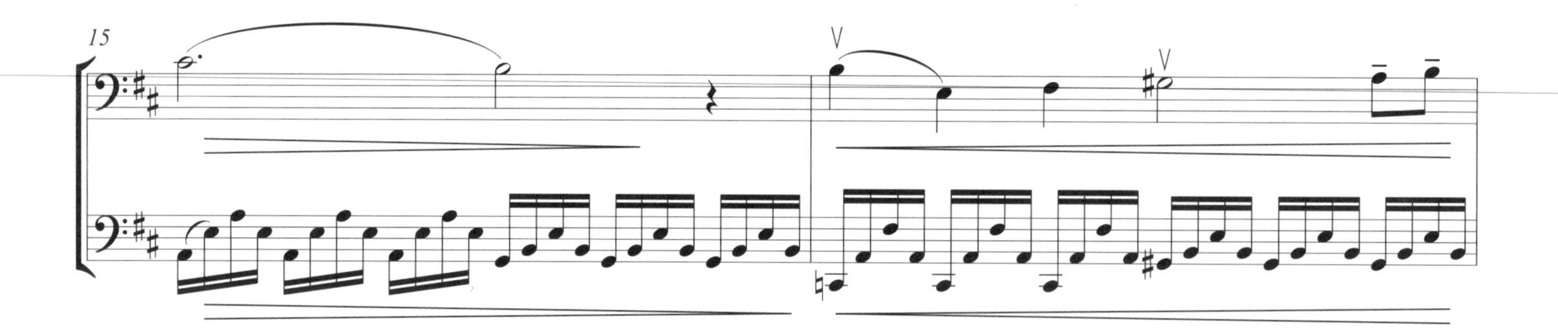
15

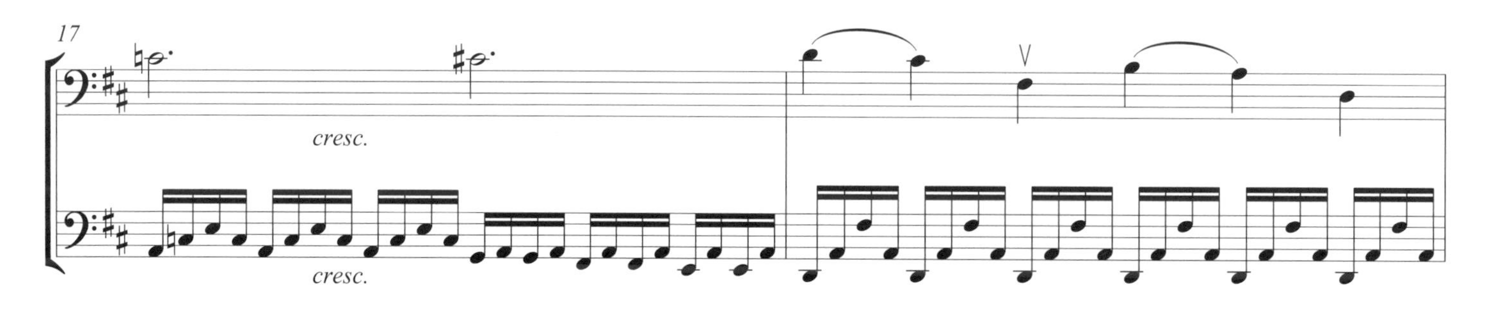
17
cresc.
cresc.

19

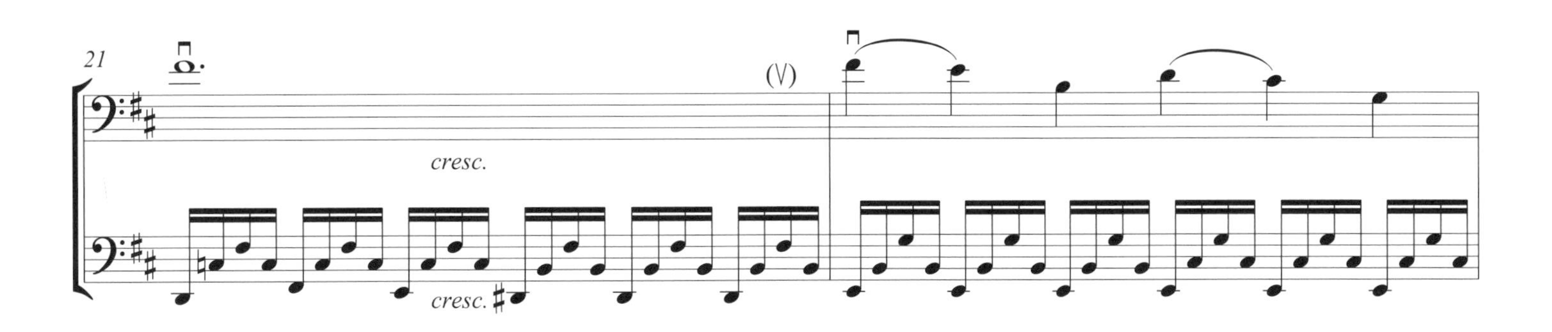
21
cresc.
cresc.

23

25
dim.

27
rit.

Va, Pensiero

from NABUCCO
By Giuseppe Verdi
Arranged by Massimiliano Martinelli and Fulvia Mancini

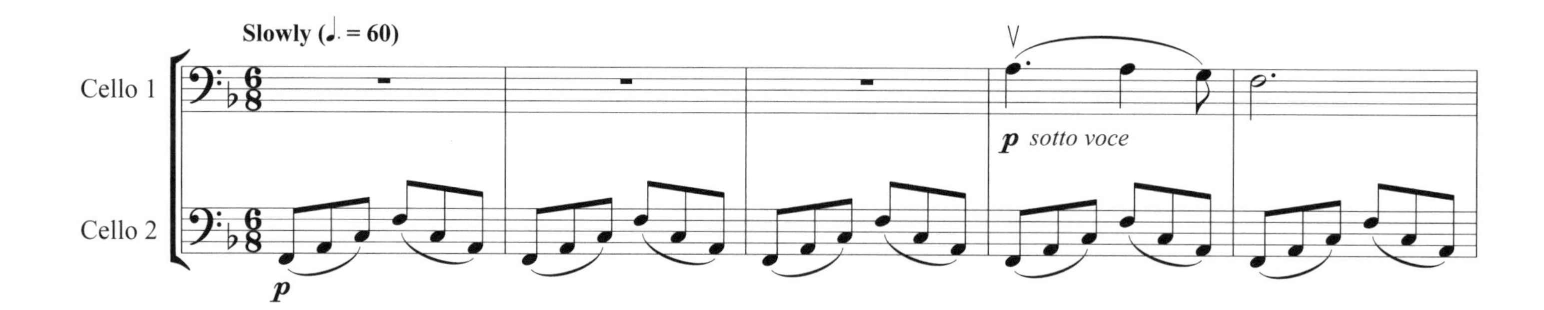

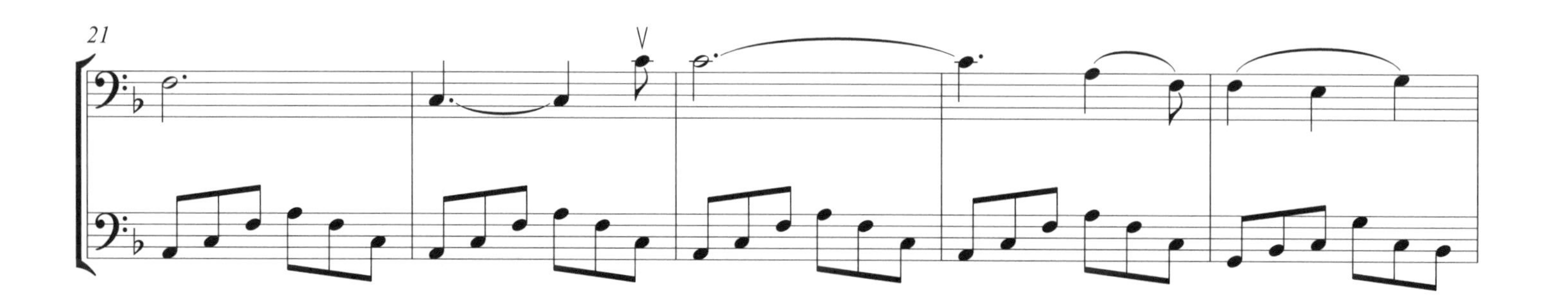

26
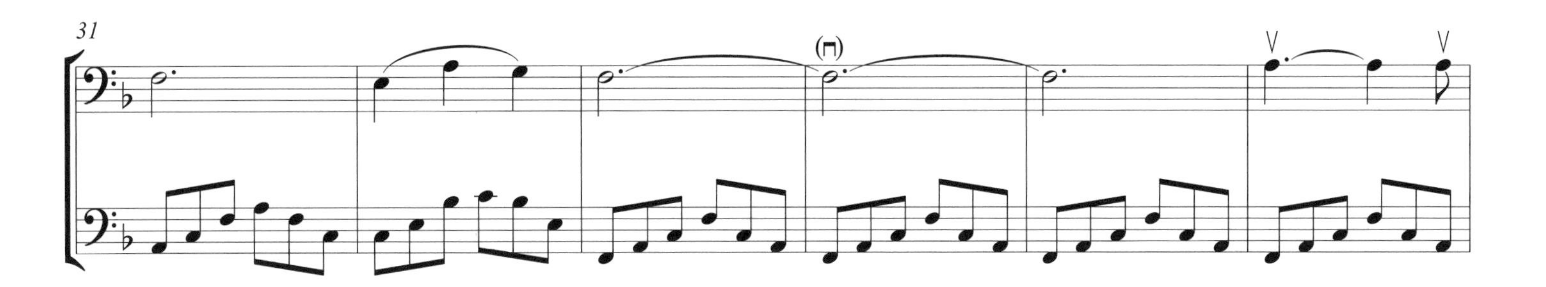
31

37

42
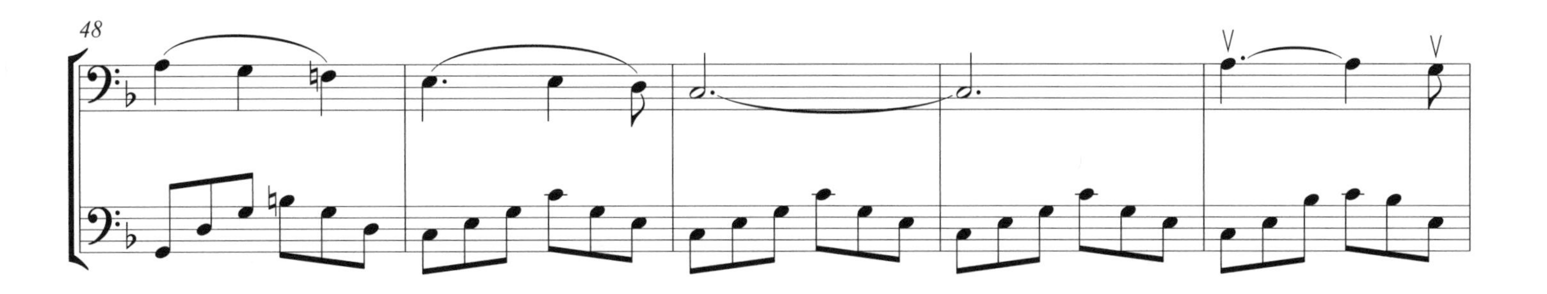
48
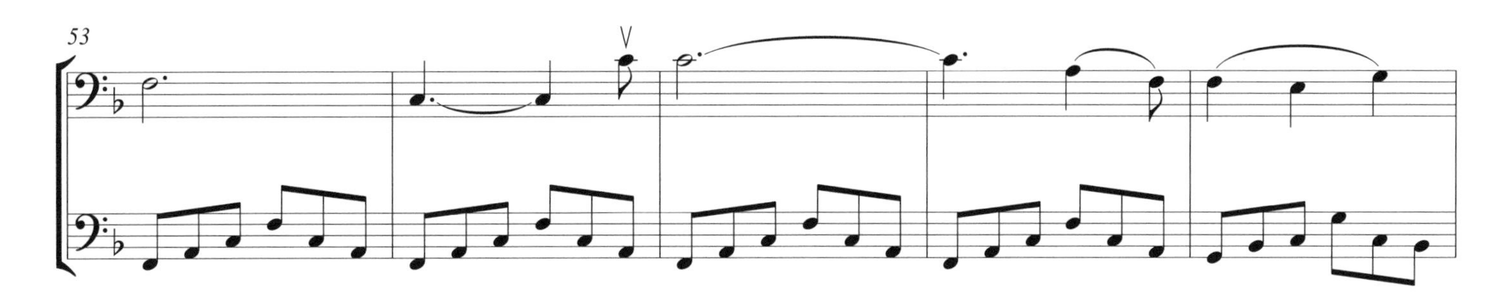
53

58

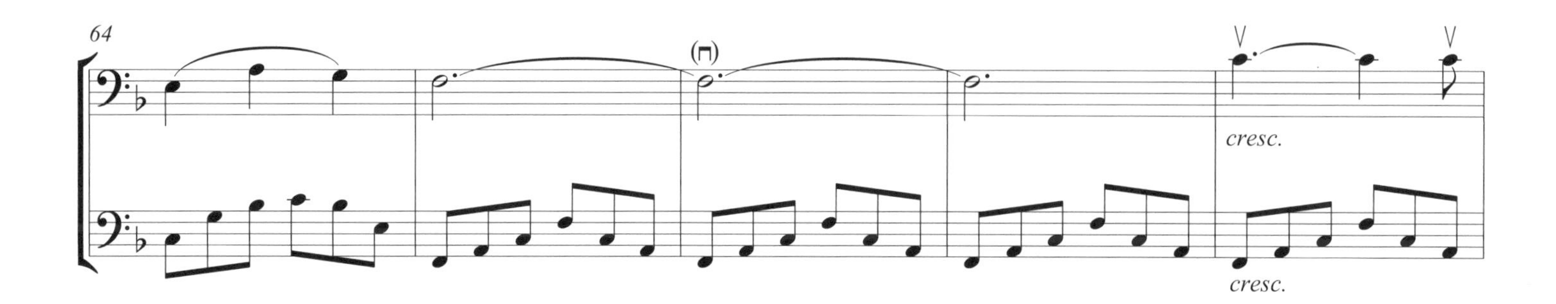
64
cresc.
cresc.

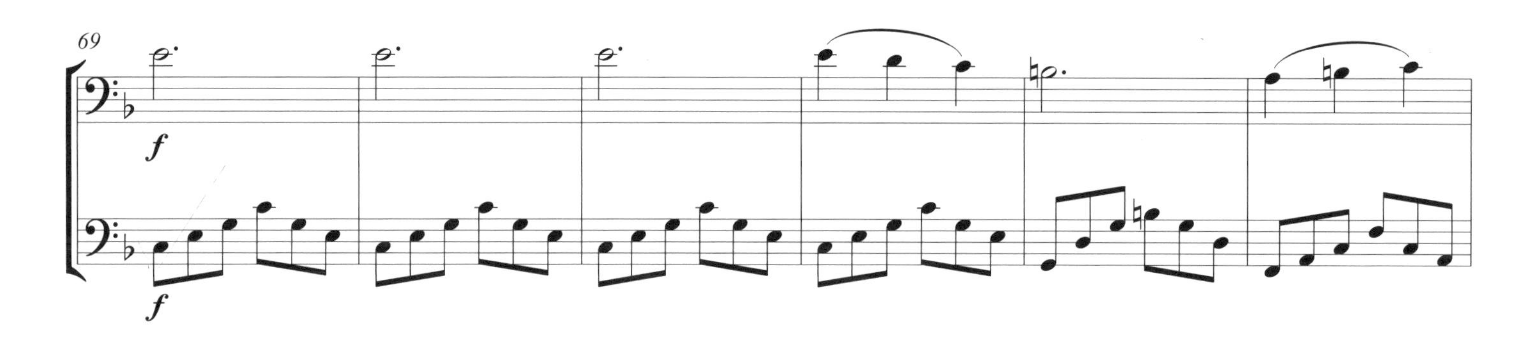
69
f
f

75
dim.
mp
dim.
mp

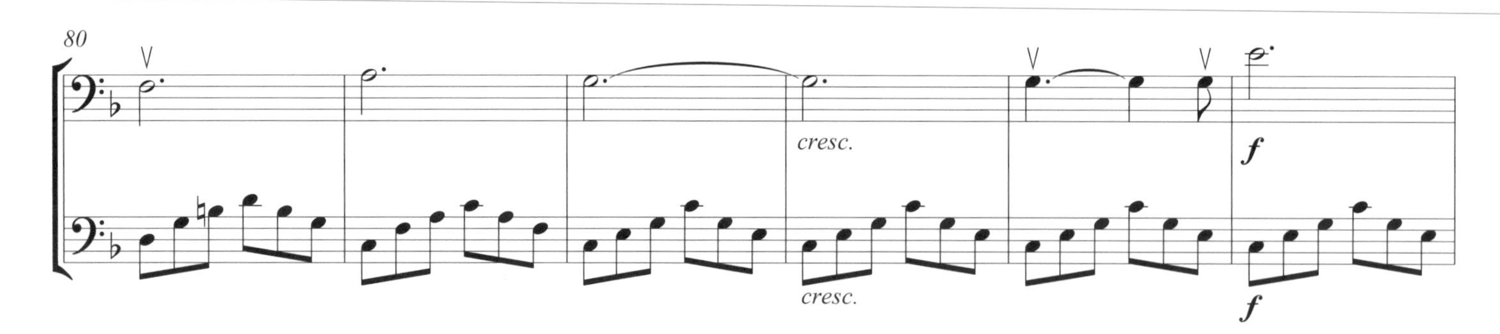
80
cresc.
f
cresc.
f

86
mf
mf

92
dim.
p
dim.
p

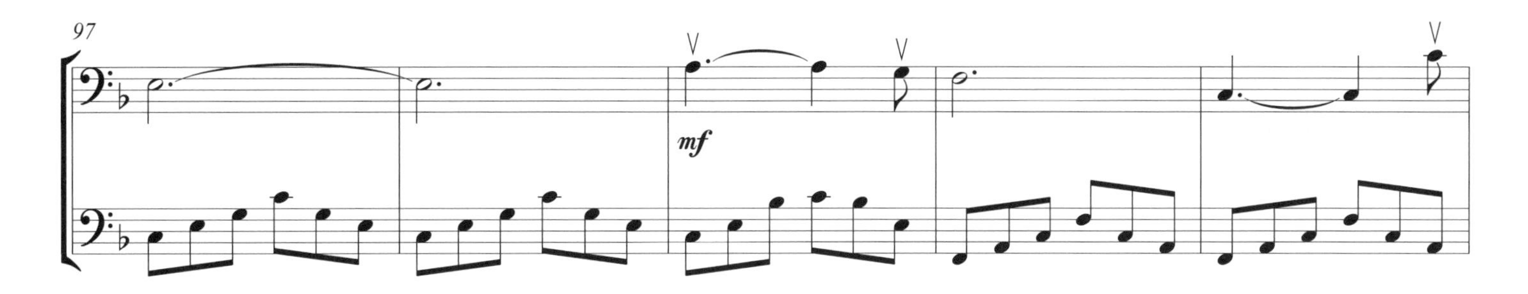
97
mf

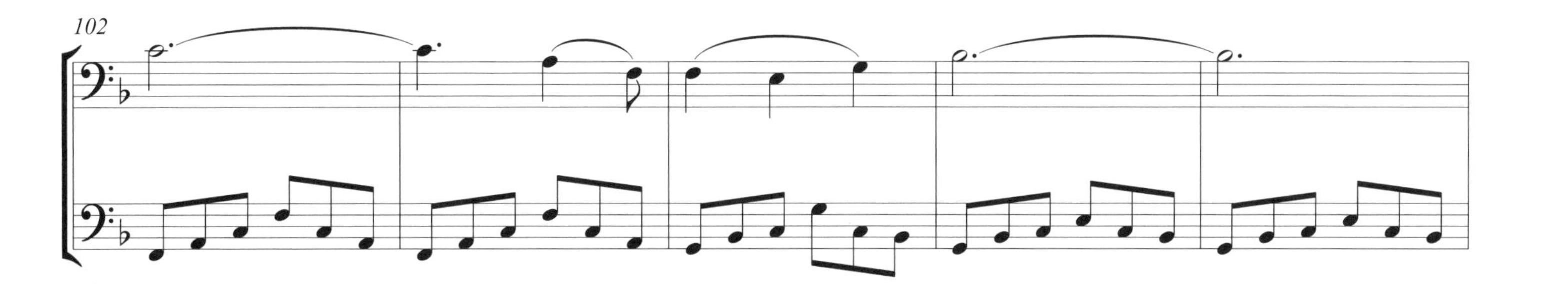
102

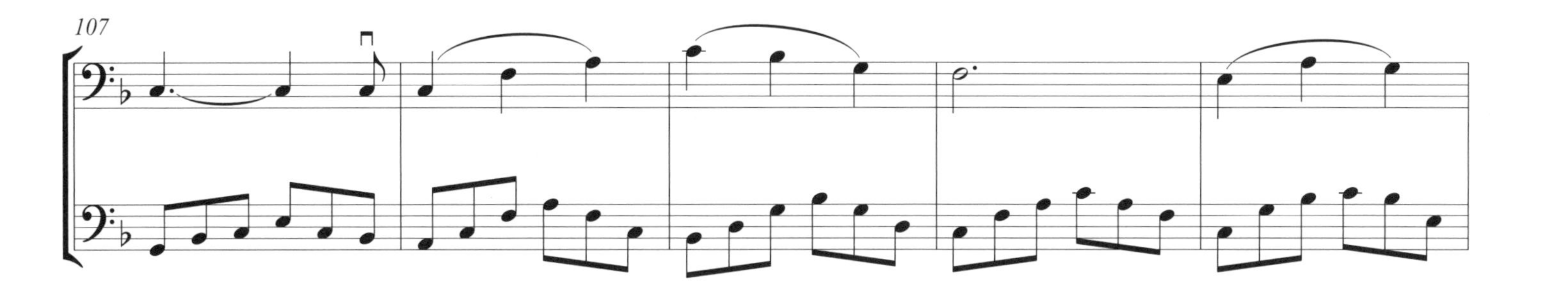
107

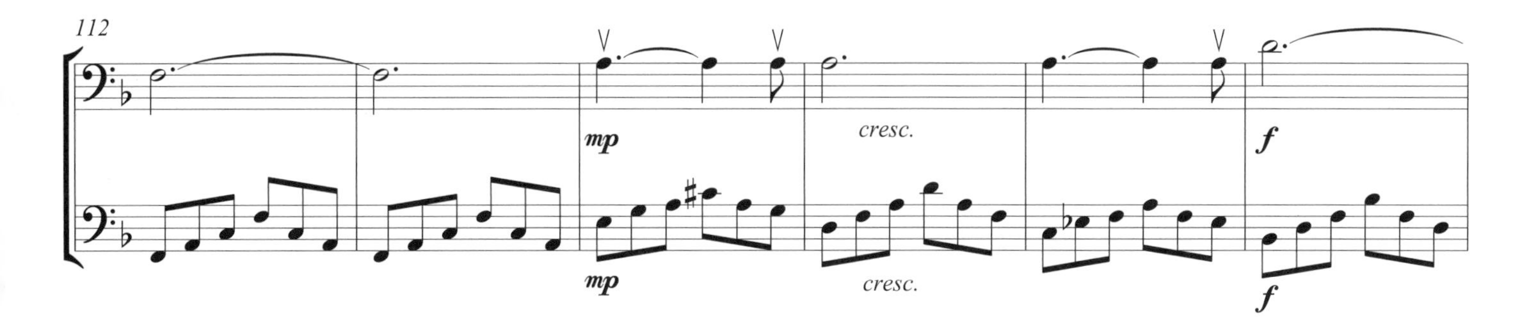
112
mp
cresc.
f
mp
cresc.
f

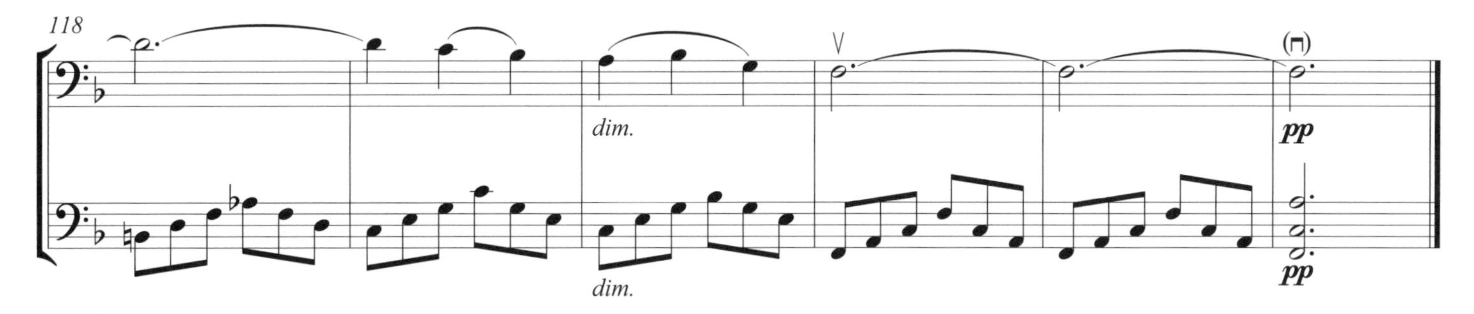
118
dim.
pp
dim.
pp

Waltz of the Flowers

from THE NUTCRACKER
By Pyotr Il'yich Tchaikovsky
Arranged by Massimiliano Martinelli and Fulvia Mancini

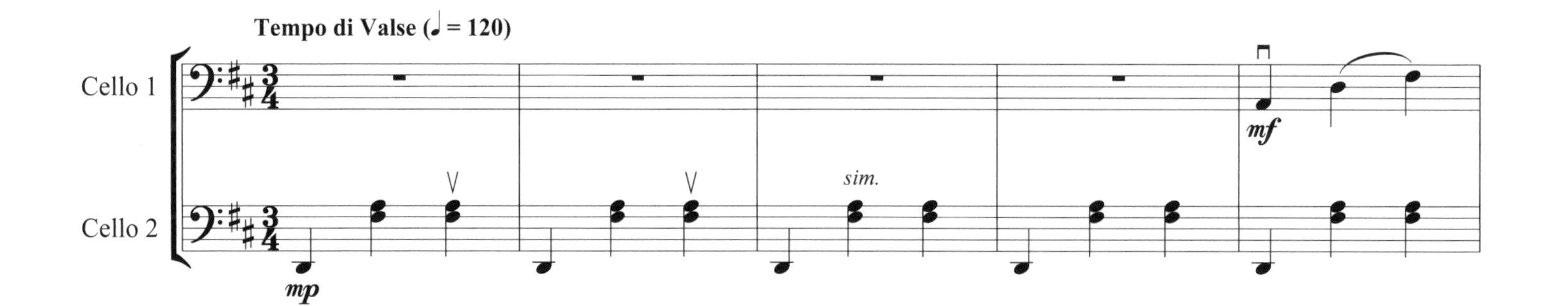

27

32
cresc.

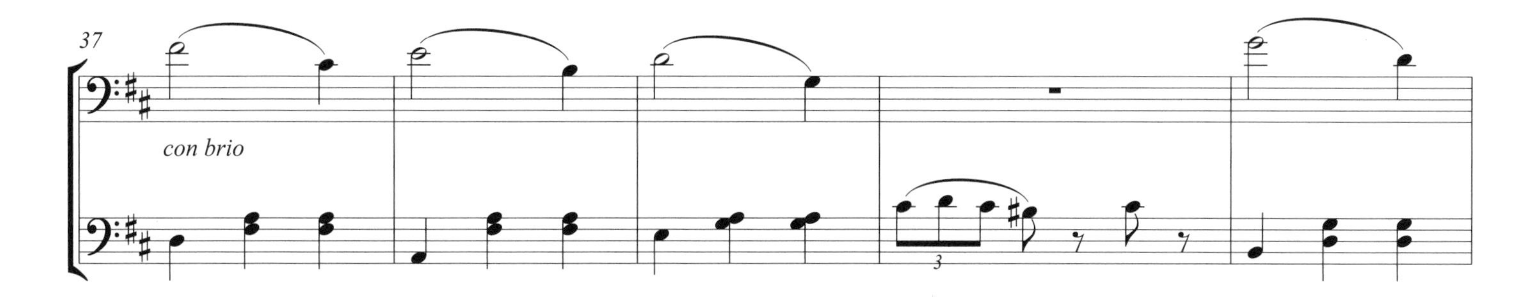
37
con brio

42

47

52

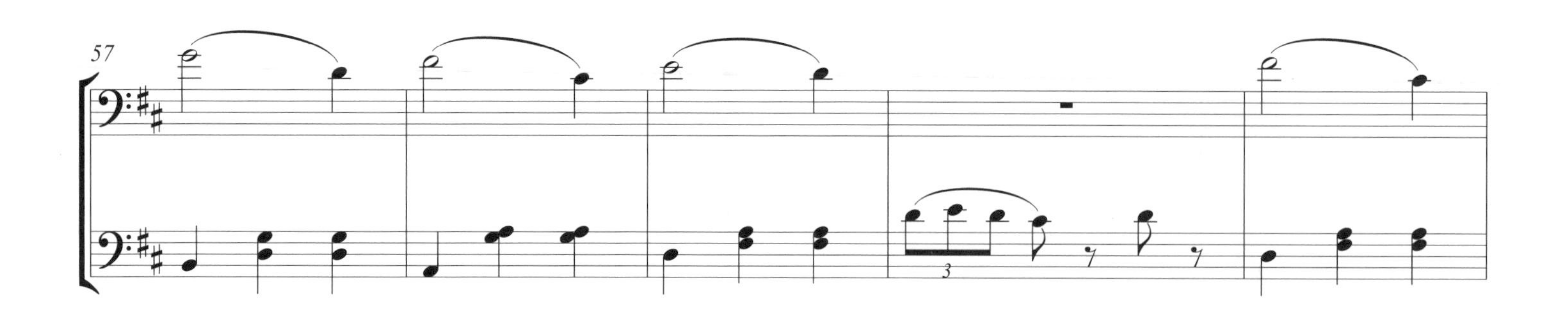
57

62

67
dolce

72

77

83
ff
f

89

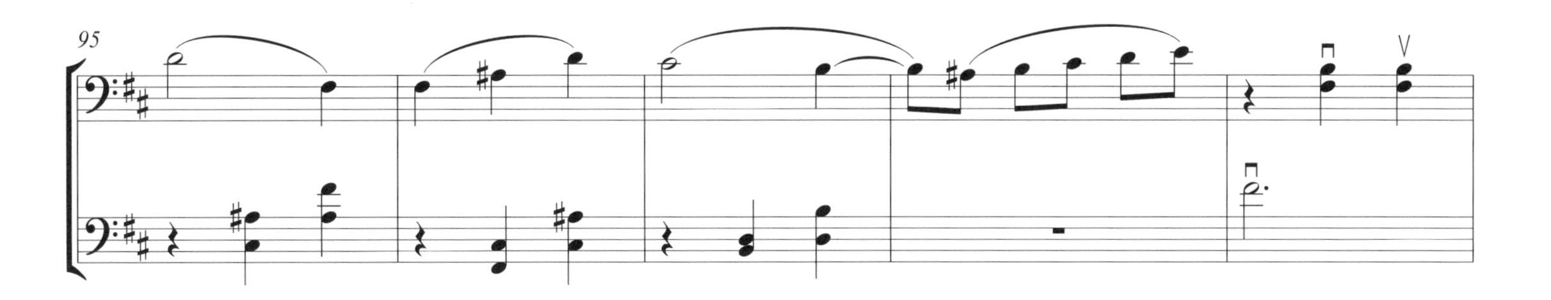
95

100

106

112
p
p

118

William Tell Overture

By Gioachino Rossini
Arranged by Massimiliano Martinelli and Fulvia Mancini

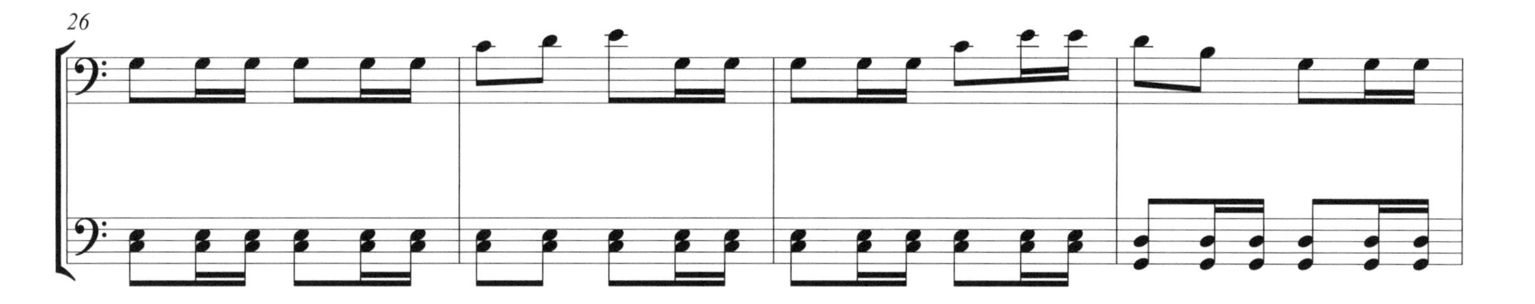
26

30

34

39

44

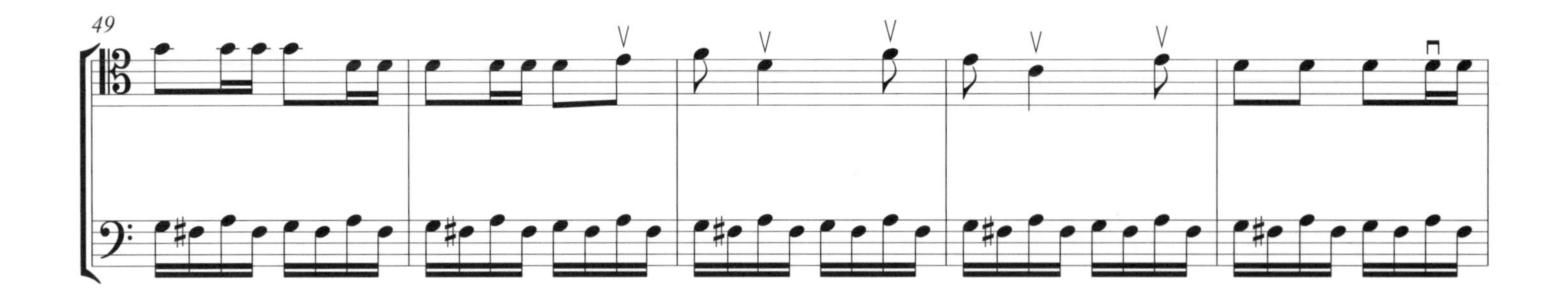
49

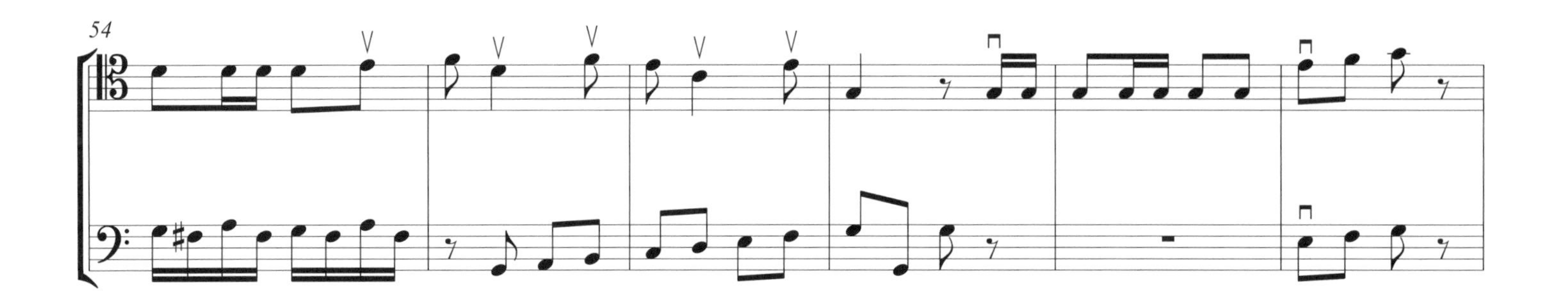
54

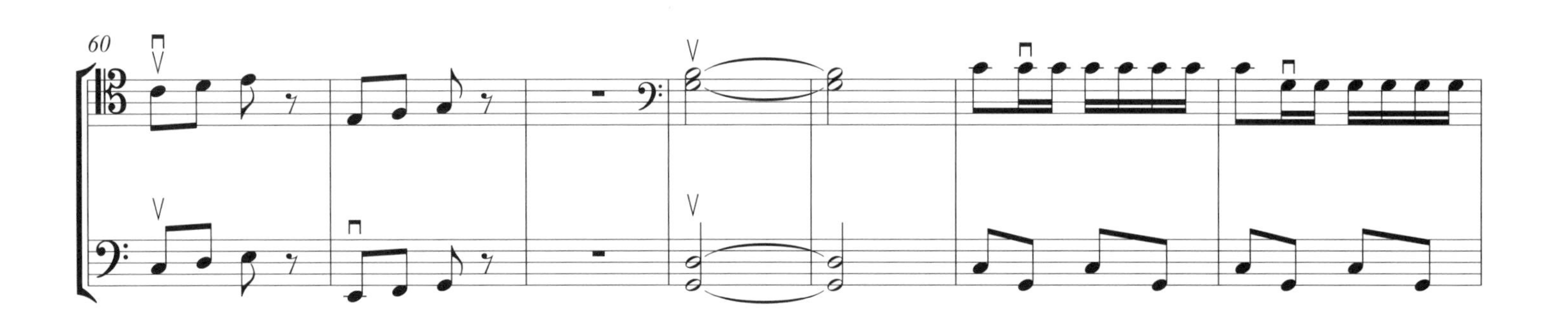
60

67

72